Herbert Wilson Griffin Seminar in International Affairs

AMERICAN DIPLOMACY IN THE INFORMATION AGE

JX
1417
.A727
1991
West

DACOR BACON HOUSE FOUNDATION

UNIVERSITY
PRESS OF
AMERICA

Lanham • New York • London

Library of Congress Cataloging-in-Publication Data

American diplomacy in the information age.
p.   cm.
"Herbert Wilson Griffin seminar in international affairs."
1. United States—Foreign relations—Congresses.
2. United States—Foreign relations—Data processing—
Congresses.   3. Information technology—Congresses.
I. University Press of America.
II. Dacor Bacon House Foundation.
JX1417.A727   1990   327.73—dc20   90–45475 CIP

ISBN 0–8191–7987–6 (cloth : alk. paper)
ISBN 0–8191–7988–4 (pbk. : alk. paper)

TABLE OF CONTENTS

iii

PREFACE

This volume is the product of a seminar, entitled American Diplomacy in the Information Age, sponsored by the Dacor Bacon House Foundation. The seminar was the second in the series of Herbert Wilson Griffin Seminars in International Affairs.

The Dacor Bacon House Foundation was established for the purpose of contributing to the development of mutual international understanding and the strengthening of ties between the people of the United States and other nations. To this end it pursues a variety of programs of a public and educational nature to enhance public awareness and foster educated leadership in the field of international affairs. Through its seminars and conferences it provides a forum for specialists to meet and exchange views on important foreign policy issues of the day. The Foundation lends direct encouragement to university-level education in international affairs by offering grants to students for advanced study in this field.

Diplomatic and Consular Officers Retired (Dacor) is an association of retired officers of the United States Foreign Service and of other foreign affairs agencies, founded in 1952 to support their interests and those of the Foreign Service. Dacor Bacon House, a historic building in Washington, D.C., is the headquarters for Dacor and the Dacor Bacon House Foundation and serves as the site for the Foundation's educational and cultural programs. It is also the home of other organizations dedicated to similar purposes.

The seminar was held at Dacor Bacon House on May 3, 1988. It was organized by the Dacor Bacon House Foundation's Program and Public Affairs Committee. Eugene Schaeffer was the project coordinator. This volume was edited by Gifford D. Malone.

INTRODUCTION

The information age has transformed the way the people of the world live and work, and the process of change continues at an accelerating pace. Computers, television and satellites, supported by advanced transmission technology have made possible instantaneous communication and unparalleled access to information. In ways too numerous to count these technological advances affect our individual daily lives, the behavior and structure of organizations, public and private, and patterns of interaction within countries and across national boundaries. Inevitably they are influencing the manner in which governments carry out their business and the nature of the problems they must address.

For people in any age to understand exactly what is happening in their own time, to find meaning in the changes taking place and to draw sensible conclusions from them is a difficult and uncertain undertaking. Nevertheless, it is obvious that changes wrought by the information age do have serious implications for relations among governments and for the way those relations are conducted. This volume represents an effort to try to understand some of these implications. It is the report of a conference whose purpose was to examine broadly the major characteristics of the information age, to attempt to see what meaning they may have for American foreign policy and diplomacy and what lessons might usefully be drawn from such an examination. This event was the second in the series designated the Herbert Wilson Griffin Seminar in International Affairs, held under the auspices of the Dacor Bacon House Foundation.

The approach taken to the subject was intentionally wide ranging. Although the effects of the information/communication revolution are evident throughout our society, relatively little effort has been devoted thus far to assessing the implications of this revolution for U.S. diplomacy. Thus, it was felt that this endeavor would be most fruitful if it were to cover the topic broadly and address a series of issues of potential importance for U.S. policy makers and diplomatic practitioners. Clearly any one of the major topics addressed in the pages that follow could be the subject of a separate, full-scale study. One hopes, indeed, that many of them will be; there is a great deal to be said and to be learned in this important area. In that respect this report is an attempt to take an early, general look at the subject, perhaps providing a basis for later, more detailed studies.

The panelists whose views are presented here represent a broad spectrum of professional expertise, both private and governmental. Their names and affiliations are listed in the following section and biographic information concerning them is given in Appendix B. They were joined in the discussion by other participants, including many former American diplomats and individuals with a variety of relevant backgrounds from outside the government. Their names are also provided in the Appendix. The proceedings were chaired by Ambassador (ret.) John Tuthill, whose expert management throughout the day-long session kept the discussion moving and focussed. The edited text, regrettably, cannot do full justice to his essential role.

With the exception of the concluding chapter, this report presents the discussion as it occurred, with appropriate editing for clarity and precision. It retains the conversational tone of the proceedings, much of whose value derived from the give and take among panelists and other participants. The report begins with an overview of global communications technology and its effects. It moves then to a discussion of the implications of these technological changes for U.S. foreign policy, with particular attention to communications, economic and political and security issues. The third section focuses on the media, with commentary by three American journalists, representing both the print media and television, upon the relationship of their spheres of activity to U.S. diplomacy. Section IV of the report deals with the conduct of American diplomacy in a global information society, with specific reference to public diplomacy, the use of technology in the Department of State and diplomatic practices overseas. The final chapter presents in summary form some of the main conclusions that emerged from the day-long proceedings.

The entire discussion, we hope, will be of interest not only to professional diplomatists, but to all those concerned with how United States foreign policy and diplomacy are able to meet the special challenges that the communications/information revolution has brought about.

Gifford D. Malone
Program and Public Affairs Committee
Dacor Bacon House Foundation

I

GLOBAL COMMUNICATIONS TECHNOLOGY: DEVELOPMENTS AND ISSUES

I

GLOBAL COMMUNICATIONS TECHNOLOGY: DEVELOPMENTS AND ISSUES

OSWALD H. GANLEY, Executive Director, Program on Information Policy and Resources, Harvard University

KENNETH W. LEESON, Telecommunications Advisor, International Business Machines Corporation

ROBERT L. CHARTRAND, Senior Specialist in Information Policy and Technology, Congressional Research Service, Library of Congress

AMBASSADOR JOHN W. TUTHILL, Seminar Chairman: The first segment of our discussion will deal with the general field of telecommunications, with some insights as to how this affects policy. We are going to try to learn as much as we can in this segment about the background of this very complicated issue.

You know the old story that it's not what you don't know that gets you into trouble. It's what you do know that's wrong. In my case there is a large area of don't know, and I think of this as an educational opportunity. I'm honored to be here with these gentlemen and the other very distinguished speakers. I congratulate the people that have organized this session and a very impressive list of participants.

Oswald Ganley will be the lead-off speaker. Dr. Ganley is the Executive Director of the Program on Information Resources and Policy at Harvard University.

DR. OSWALD H. GANLEY: Mr. Ambassador, thank you very much. As a former Foreign Service officer, it is a particular pleasure for me to be here and to have the privilege of talking a little about the implications of some of these communications and information issues in foreign policy.

1

I will start by reading a very succinct description of a seminar series on the foreign policy and security issues of communications and information that I will be teaching this coming fall at the Center for International Affairs at Harvard. Then I will go into it and try to break down the subject.

Rapid changes are underway in the world of telecommunications, computers and information which have critical implications for the well being of the industrialized nations, the NICs and the LDCs and which figure prominently in the future plans of the socialist countries. These changes influence economies, competitiveness, trade relations and internal and external politics, including those concerning unrest, revolution and terrorism. They impact heavily on warfare and national security through shifts in weapon systems, command control and intelligence collection and dissemination and security. The conduct of diplomacy and the role of the embassy and the ambassador have also been profoundly shaken.

I do not consider this description an exaggeration of the changes that are already underway and that we can expect over the next decade or so. Let me break the subject down into such things as the telephone, the computer, television, VCRs, super computers and a few other categories.

The telephone. Let's begin with the telephone. It is perhaps the simplest. We all know how to use it, although very few of us understand the real workings behind it. Every child can pick it up. Everybody can talk into it.

The important thing behind the telephone, however, is the network, and it is the network that is causing the many changes that we deal with on a day-to-day basis. This network can be used not just for voice transmission, although even today 85 percent of the revenue of the telephone system, both domestically and internationally, comes from voice uses, not from fancy things like data communications or a computer talking to a computer. In fact, at one time there was a company that spent hundreds of millions of dollars setting up a fantastic satellite system, thinking that all kinds of computers wanted to talk to other computers, and that people really didn't want to talk to each other. To their surprise, it wasn't so. They ended up going back to plain old voice and decided to write off their losses.

The modern telecommunications network behind the telephone is essential for financial services and for multi-national corporations. It is also a basic part of the national security system. Some 85 to 90 percent of all military traffic, including that of the most sensitive nature, goes through the same ordinary telephone network that you and I use.

This presents certain problems. The ordinary network is used by business, and sometimes the most sensitive technical subjects are discussed or information transferred in the form of data through these open networks. The question then is: Who else listens to this telephone? If one believes the Rockefeller report of a number of years ago, and I certainly do, "if you don't want it to be known, don't use the telephone." Of course, those of us who have worked in classified areas know very well all the signs that say "don't use the telephone."

This is a very real problem and one that needs to be further considered. The Reagan administration, particularly, has been concerned about these things with regard to civilians. So we got National Security Decision Memorandum 145, which said we ought to be protecting the civilian network. This again presents a problem, namely, who will protect it? The original idea was that the National Security Agency, in other words, the military, the Department of Defense, would secure civilian telephones. But many civilians don't want the military, in any form or manner, to control the civilian network or to tell civilians what they can or cannot do. Then people came up with the idea of a "cheap scrambling type of telephone." Well, there are still certain problems of who would control such a system.

On the diplomatic side, the telephone also presents some interesting questions. First, secure phones are very scarce items. Second, the telephone is increasingly being used for communications. Many ambassadors and other senior people in embassies consider this as *the* way to communicate with Washington, thinking that this way there will be no record. One of the problems with that idea is that nothing prevents someone from taping the message. This raises some very interesting questions of "command and control" between the field and policy-makers in Washington.

The changes in the telephone have been so extensive that it has now become a trade issue. For instance, the United States pushed the Japanese very hard to do something about the monopoly of the Nippon Telephone and Telegraph (NTT). And we ourselves, in this country, because of the various changes and because of the importance to the economy, decided to break up AT&T. This may have been a good idea or a bad one. The jury is still out. But, in any case, this change has created a tremendous number of major policy issues about what to do and what not to do. Major things are now happening in the European Communities as the EC considers removing all the internal barriers in 1992. What to do about the telephone networks, who can use them, and under what conditions? Who will have the comparative advantage? These are major questions which diplomacy is going to have to deal with.

Finally, with regard to modern diplomacy generally, American diplomats are not usually trained to work in the area of regulatory policy. This is left to specialists. But there are some very important policy questions involved here of a political and economic nature. If you do not understand at least the basics of regulatory mechanisms, then as senior diplomats you are at a major disadvantage -- that is, you are at the mercy of the specialists and the lawyers who manipulate the regulatory process as they like.

The computer. Without the computer there would be no information business as we have come to know it. It is the base. It can be anything from a monster at least the size of a large room to a microchip that is one or two millimeters square. The microchip is nothing but a computer. A computer is simply something that can manipulate data in one way or other, that works with zeros and ones, and that has an on and off switch.

Computers are a very profitable business for the United States. This is one of the very few areas where the U.S. enjoys a trade surplus, which was $7.5 billion in 1987. U.S. companies have approximately 72 percent of the world's total computer business. The U.S. has about 70 percent of the software market of the world. There are, however, certain clouds on the horizon. Namely, in a number of years, this balance of trade may shift to the negative, just as it has in the telephone area.

Television. Again, it is a very simple instrument. We all know it. We use it every day. But it has created some very interesting issues in diplomacy, especially regarding the role of the press and real-time reporting. Those of you who have arranged a presidential visit are well aware that the President will arrive just on time at the airport so that the evening news, or the seven o'clock morning news, will catch the arrival of the great man. Everybody knows about it instantly, in real time. Even His Holiness, the Pope, will arrive at a certain place in Africa on the exact moment, so that the event will get on the evening or the morning television. This matter of immediate, real time news has a major influence on how such trips will be handled.

Through television and the satellite, it is now possible to broadcast directly into the Soviet Union. As a matter of fact, there is now a television station in Luxembourg which has such a large footprint -- that is the area where it beams -- that it goes directly into the Soviet Union. It is my understanding that Soviet citizens take advantage of this. They can buy certain electronic parts or use chicken wire to make dish antennas. They pick up the signal even though this particular one is not very powerful. It is not a direct broadcasting satellite, but a satellite with just an ordinary transponder.

The VCR. The VCR is an extraordinarily interesting development. My wife has spent the last two years working on the VCR and its global political implications. The VCR can be very easily used for all kinds of political messages. It can be smuggled in by one means or another. It is all over Eastern Europe. It is all over the Soviet Union. It is all over the Middle East. In the smallest villages in India you can find a VCR. Most are used for pure entertainment, and a little bit of pornography is thrown in here and there. But they are also very usable for political messages of one kind or another. They were rather extensively used in the overthrow of Marcos in the Philippines. They have been used in Nicaragua, in El Salvador, and in all sorts of political situations.

A new technology that has equally interesting possibilities is just starting to be used, for instance, in the attempts to overthrow Mr. Noriega in Panama. This is the combination of "Mac and Fax," a very interesting brotherhood. The Mac is the Macintosh computer, and the Fax, of course, is facsimile. There is an organization right in Washington which collects newspaper articles, translates them into

Spanish and sets them up as a newspaper on the Macintosh. They are then thrown into a facsimile machine, which sends them off quite cheaply to Panama. There are lots of facsimile machines in Panama, for a variety of reasons. Once in Panama the news items are thrown into a reproduction machine, and then they are distributed. It is a major operation, reasonably well financed, and it is very effective. That is the latest use of technology for purposes of this nature.

Satellites. Satellites are, of course, used for communications satellites and give us a communications abundance. Other interesting aspects of satellites are their uses for purpose of sensing, spying, taking photographs, picking up telemetry, and so on. These days it is a very open business.

Open sensing started out with LANDSAT. For civilian purposes we are allowed in the United States to sense at not less than 30 meters resolution. But then came competition. The French launched a commercial sensing satellite called SPOT in 1986, and they started to sell items at ten meters resolution. Of course with ten meters resolution you can see very much more than with 30. But the U.S. government continued to say to LANDSAT, "no, no, you can't do that. "The military and the security people said terrible things would happen if civilians should get their hands on such materials. To make matters worse the Soviets said they were going to sell five meter resolution pictures. They offered them to U.S. private sources and also to the U.S. government. They are available for every place except the Soviet Union. The Soviets will sell you five meter resolution pictures of any other country.

The important point in all this is that the media are looking at the question of acquiring their own so-called "Mediasat." With their own satellite it will be possible for the media to watch what is going on directly. During the Chernobyl disaster, for instance, the first pictures of what was happening and the real extent of the damage became known through the commercial use of the French SPOT, as well as LANDSAT.

One consequence of higher resolution will be that civilians will be able to pick up troop concentrations -- our troop concentrations or somebody else's. So lying, or providing misinformation or disinformation from capitals will become a little bit more difficult as time goes on.

I hope I have given you a little sense of the fact that these various things we hear about have important implications for trade, for national security, for the military and for diplomacy.

AMBASSADOR TUTHILL: Thank you very much. The second speaker is Dr. Kenneth Leeson, Telecommunications Advisor of IBM.

DR. KENNETH W. LEESON: Thank you very much, Mr. Ambassador. In my comments I will be embellishing many of the issues that Ozzie mentioned. What I hope to do is set out a kind of a mental picture of the scope of the field that we are dealing with here, and one that fits in very well with the comments we have already heard. Then I would like to conclude by raising a number of questions that I believe capture some of the key issues that we are going to have to deal with in international diplomacy in the information age between now and the turn of the century.

There are two reasons for my being a participant in this discussion. One is that I work for IBM, a company that is in the eye of the storm of the information revolution. It has a great stake in how U.S. diplomacy is conducted in this field. It is a high tech company and it generates something in the neighborhood of $50 billion in revenue every year, which is larger than the gross national product perhaps of some countries. IBM relies very heavily on the free flow of information to conduct its business. It requires also a very strong cost-based telecommunications infrastructure to successfully reach its customers. It is certainly strongly affected by the policies of other governments. IBM operates in scores of countries around the world. As a matter of fact, somewhere in the neighborhood of 50 percent of the corporation's revenues is generated by its activities in foreign countries. So it obviously has a stake, and that is one of the reasons IBM is happy to have me come down and say a few words to you.

In my current job, just to lend a little illustration, my responsibilities pertain to promoting liberalization in the telecommunications industries in countries around the world. That is what I do on a day-to-day basis. This activity is not too dissimilar from some of the responsibilities that I had when I was with the government.

In the late 1970s and early 1980s when I joined the government in an advisory capacity, we saw the emergence of several issues and a lot of change, coming at a time when the question of the size and significance of information began to be widely debated. There was the north-south debate on how newly emerging countries were going to share in the fruits of the information age. They did not want to be left behind, as they argued that they had been in the industrial age. We heard talk about a new world information and communications order. There was concern about what was called transborder data flow, that is, the movement of large amounts of information from computers in one country to computers in another country and how this might affect issues such as personal privacy. Then there was, of course, the growth of the services industries and the fact that a lot more of our economic activity has come to rely on information and its free flow.

We also noticed that many of the policies that we were pursuing were not up to the task or that there really was no cogent U.S. policy in this area. Thus, there has been and there continues to be a lot of activity in the U.S. government in trying to establish policy. As a matter of fact, a few years ago, before I left the State Department, Secretary Shultz called together a small group of individuals and asked the very questions that we are talking about here. What are the major issues? What are the big questions that foreign policy is going to have to grapple with in the information age?

A few of us decided that the best way to handle this was to write an inter-office memo, just the typical bureaucratic response to a request like that. After composing it, I dropped it in the inter-office mail just as I left the State Department three years ago.

Let me say before getting into the particulars just a few words about the process involved here. Diplomacy is the province of generalists, individuals who must have a grasp of a broad range of topics. Communications and information, however, are the domain of specialists. So what we have seen, I think, in the U.S. government in the last decade or so is a flood of specialists coming into the field of diplomacy in one way or another, supporting the activities that diplomats have traditionally carried. This has spawned a great deal of activity. In fact, one can count 15 different agencies in the federal government that have some responsibility for one or another of the issues that we are going to be talking about in this conference.

Now, how do you line up all of these agencies, point them in the right direction and get them to speak with a single voice? That has been a very difficult problem, though I think, again, some progress has been made. There have been efforts to coordinate the government in the last few years. A single agency simply cannot do it all. A single individual simply cannot do it all. As a matter of fact, the State Department created a bureau to try to coordinate U.S. policy in this area, a bureau that I was involved with while I was at the State Department.

What is the setting for diplomacy in the information age? I will give one rendition here. First of all, we know that communications and information are growing in economic significance. Over 50 percent of the income of industrialized countries can be attributed to some form of information activity today. We have satellite technology, fiber optics, and many of the technologies that Ozzie Ganley reviewed, increasing communications capacity. Transmission capacity is no longer a constraint. It is far less expensive to use and move information today than at any time in the past. Computers are linked to computers around the world. While the proportion of total traffic attributable to "non-voice" communication is, at the moment, small, it is growing, and we can expect it to grow dramatically. And it may well raise some problems.

IBM has done a "sizing of the industry" at the international level and has come up with a figure, excluding information content, on the order of $550 billion for the world-wide market in 1986. This includes information machines such as computers and telecommunications equipment, value added network services, and the underlying transport networks. This figure is expected to grow, according to this estimate, at an 11 percent annual rate, which will bring it to over a trillion dollars by 1992. So you can see it is a rather significant field, and it is growing rapidly.

Secondly, in addition to the industry's size, there is the accelerating pace of technological change. A very good example of how this affects policy can be found in our own country. The Federal Communications Commission has, for the last 20 years, been undertaking an ongoing review of its regulatory approach to traditional carriers in this country. It has always tried to determine the best way to regulate, or abstain from regulating, the emerging information activities that are very much related to telecommunications. It is a constantly changing scene requiring constant attention.

As an illustration of the changing pace of technology, I have some figures on the increase in the efficiency of the computer. In 1955, it cost $14.54 and took 375 seconds to complete 1,700 standard data processing operations, a basket of operations including mathematical manipulation and movement of information from processor to memory, etc. By 1985 the same 1,700 operations cost 4 cents and took four-tenths of a second to accomplish, 364 times as cheap and 938 times as fast. The ground is clearly shifting beneath our feet here.

The third point, in addition to size and rapid technological changes, is the fact that governments around the world all respond in a different way to these changes, yet communications must be maintained. That is the diplomatic question: How do we interact with these other governments? The process can be characterized as follows: Rapid technological change creates opportunities internationally. Enterprises, governments and individuals all move to exploit the opportunities that technology brings about. Governments look at the information age and information economies as a strategic interest. They may not like the way entities exploit and adjust to the technology, so they amend the rules. They do so domestically and they do so internationally. This creates a new setting, new opportunities, new exploitation of opportunities, and again the adjustment cycle repeats itself. Diplomacy in the information age is a matter of chasing this cycle.

To illustrate the scope of the field itself, let me try quickly to draw a mental picture to give some idea of the vastness of the subject matter we are dealing with. Imagine a continuum beginning at one extreme with the underlying technology and moving to the other extreme of information content. Along this continuum several issues are raised. To begin with the technology, we can identify issues pertaining to the equipment the technology makes possible -- information equipment, such as computers. The equipment is produced and then interconnected into networks according to certain technological rules that are promulgated internationally. The networks provide telecommunications and information services. These services themselves raise issues, such as trade rules that should apply. The services make possible the flow of information itself, and the flow of information affects the policies and objectives of governments. Very briefly, this spectrum of issues is what we are talking about when we talk about diplomacy in the information age.

To be more specific, when one looks at technology, for example, we think of science policy. We think of the need for indigenous national capacities to produce technology in the information age. These are questions that governments are concerned with. We also think of the transfer of technology. There are policies on each of these that require our attention.

In the equipment sector, governments seek to develop domestic industrial capacity. Everybody wants to be a player in the information age -- all industrialized countries, certainly, want to have strong indigenous capacities for producing computers and switches and other components of the industry. These machines are then woven into a structure, and governments have to speak to governments on questions of facilities planning.

International communications is a two-way street. There must be rules of the road that specify, for example, how AT&T meets British Telecom in the middle of the Atlantic, so that we can communicate over the circuits. Numerous services are then provided by these facilities. Banking is an obvious example. The banking industry relies increasingly on international communication facilities that are set up to conduct its business. Furthermore, much else in commerce depends on the health and efficiency of the banking industry. The information flowing over the networks raises a number of questions, such as press freedom, restrictions on journalists, and privacy protection. There is a great deal of information about each of us in computers in the United States and perhaps around the world. How can we be sure that people don't have unauthorized access to that information, for commercial purposes or any other reasons? We may also have to grapple with questions of property rights as they pertain to information. Information is intangible, of a different substance than hardware, yet it has value. How can we protect that value? Then there is the question of surveillance of content which Ozzie mentioned earlier.

This is one rendition of the scope of the field, and some of the issues that concern governments. The international process of diplomacy is really a matter of chasing after these issues.

Let me conclude by summarizing the contents of the memo that I mentioned earlier. We decided to break down the field -- the big questions of the day -- into five major issues. One was national sovereignty and state control; the second, international institutions and diplomacy; the third, freedom of expression, privacy and surveillance; the fourth, economic questions, particularly the value of information in international commerce; and finally, diplomacy and the law. I will give a sampling of the kinds of questions that were proposed just a few years ago, those that would have to be given attention, certainly between now and the turn of the century. I would also note that these questions, on a day-to-day basis, ebb and flow in their relative significance -- yesterday's hot issue may be cold today and warm tomorrow.

On the question of national sovereignty and state control: Will communication technologies lead inevitably to a greater flow of information among citizens of the world or will countervailing technologies of control frustrate such developments? We hear a lot of talk about the so-called technological imperative. Governments are not going to be able to control information because there will be so many channels. Technology will not permit control. That may be true, but only to a certain extent.

Will greater access to information weaken the sovereignty of governments, promoting political change or instability in countries? Will such forces affect U.S. interests positively or negatively?

International institutions and diplomacy: There have been serious indications, certainly in the early part of this decade, of a deterioration in the effectiveness with which international organizations carry out their mandated functions, particularly regarding communications resources. What will be the relevance of these organizations in future years? How can we make them more responsive to our interests? One might cite UNESCO as an example. Are we seeing a shift from multilateralism to bilateralism?

One example of where some of these issues may be a concern is in the organization principally responsible, internationally, for telecommunications issues: the International Telecommunications Union in Geneva. Here, the United States has, in the past couple of years, had troublesome political problems, and this in an organization that is supposed to be devoted to technical solutions. At the moment, there seems to be a quiescent period in that regard, but there are meetings coming up in the next five years in which we might see a return to some of the political rhetoric that we have heard in such organizations in the past.

Also under institutions and diplomacy: Private enterprise relies on market forces and minimal government involvement, familiar characteristics of communications policy in the U.S. In most other countries, however, communications activities are closely controlled by government and government-owned monopolies, whose motivations and objectives are very different than those of private firms in the United States. Given these significant differences, what will be the most effective strategies and policies for the U.S. to pursue in attempting to attain its foreign policy objectives? We are making good progress, I would say, in trying to persuade other countries that the time is right to change some of their policies, some of the restrictive policies pertaining to their telecommunications industries.

Are existing international treaty arrangements in communications out of date? If so, what does this imply for long-term U.S. policy? An example I might cite is the international satellite organization, INTELSAT, and the U.S. initiative three to five years ago to permit competition with what had been by treaty a monopoly on international telecommunications satellite services. That institution has gone through important changes and is still trying to accept and absorb the kinds of changes that technology is permitting.

How can the best balance be struck between commitment on the one hand and flexibility on the other in international treaties, particularly in light of the changes in the field? It is very difficult for countries to get together and write a list of rules about the information age, because it changes every day. It would be outdated by the time the ink is dry. Another example of this is a current activity in the World Administrative Telegraph and Telephone Conference, which is seeking to write a series of rules on the way telecommunications services are provided -- that is, rules pertaining to the networks -- but will also consider regulations about the services provided over these networks.

We must also look at freedom of expression, privacy and surveillance. Advancing technologies bring with them both the capacity to support free expression through an increase in communications channels and diversity of content, as well as the potential to control or censor the content by increasing the means of monitoring or manipulating the channels.

The fourth topic is the value of information in international commerce. At the moment we do not have rules of the road in services internationally under a General Agreeement on Trade and Taffifs (GATT) regime, as we do in merchandise. Much of the post-war era was spent trying to reduce barriers to merchandise trade under the auspices of the GATT. Now there is an effort underway to do something similar for services. In my reading of the activity to date there is not unanimity internationally among countries about how the GATT should handle these questions. I think this is a very important question to be addressed over the next several years.

Finally, there are the legal issues that have to be grappled with--liability, choice of law, extraterritoriality, intellectual property. Just to give one example, with the spread of information networks traversing multiple national boundaries, tying together widely dispersed computers, how will liability for economic loss due to human or system error be determined? Which laws will apply, and how will problems of extraterritorial application of national laws be adjudicated?

That concludes my comments on the scope of the field. I hope you find this helpful as a backdrop to the issues raised throughout the later discussion.

AMBASSADOR TUTHILL: Thank you very much, Dr. Leeson, and especially for that hopeful dream of the 17 agencies in the Executive Branch who are going to speak with a single voice at some future time. I hope they are moving in that direction.

Let's go right over to Robert Chartrand, who is from the Congressional Research Service at the Library of Congress, where he is Senior Fellow Specialist on Information Policy and Technology.

ROBERT L. CHARTRAND: We have all heard and considered the kaleidoscopic issues that Ken has run through and the fact that these, of course, do receive what I guess we could at best call "mixed reviews", depending on the sector that you're talking to. It almost becomes a situation very much like the one that Talleyrand commented upon many, many years ago -- a man of another diplomatic service -- when he was reflecting on a particularly attractive young woman of general, far-flung acquaintance. He said, "There is a lot to say in her favor, but the other is far more interesting."

I always start from the position not of cynicism but one that I would like to think is pragmatic. The statistics that you have heard from both Ken and Oz tell us why Congress as an entity and in its individual components must be interested *and* involved in this very, very convoluted area. One of the looks that was taken at the issue some five years ago by my colleague Jane Bortnick, was a report prepared for the Senate Committee on Foreign Relations, entitled "International Telecommunications and Information Policy: Selected Issues for the 1980s." Without placing any burden on my colleague, I daresay that the time will come before too long when there is going to be a need for a revision, a fresh look at those same issues, as well as other key issues and elements for the 1990's. That is really in part why we are here at this conference.

What we are saying, then, is that we live in a world of what Winston Churchill characterized as "wizard machines". I always liked that phrase, for that is the way I feel about them sometimes! Maybe that is because I am a person of Jeffersonian ideals. What we find is that we have in our country -- unlike some other countries -- a necessary and effective combination of private and public sector role players, and that simply is not true in terms of other national private sector groups. We find that the computer, and the "information," and the telecommunication industries, as you well know, all compete in an open marketplace. I think that this must be one of our cardinal thoughts as we consider this area. It is sometimes an uneasy partnership. It is also fair for those of us that have been around the Washington scene for a long time to say that the relationship between the Executive and Legislative branches of the federal government also is sometimes a bit on the uneasy side, but there has to be a working relationship between them. I would like to comment briefly on some of these aspects.

People have observed that Congress is a labyrinth, and I think that might be a fair characterization, particularly when you consider the number of oversight groups that either pretend to have or actually have cognizance over some of the activities in the State Department, Department of Commerce, Office of the U.S. Trade Representative, or even such special groups as the Senior Interagency Group on International Communications and Information Policy. The last is an especially important one. You find that there is a difficulty of role definition wherein the congressional elements -- the committees, subcommittees, special caucuses, and the individual members -- are concerned, because you have overlapping and often conflicting jurisdictions.

There have been some members both on the present scene and in the past who have taken special interest in some of these evolving circumstances that we consider today, particularly where the impact of technology is concerned -- yet, not as many members or staff people as a lot of us would like. You have had a few outstanding members such as Richard Bolling and John Brademas, and some of you I hope remember Bradford Morse, who later on went to the United Nations, and the late Bill Stieger. Today on the scene we have people like Bill Bradley and Al Gore, who are very knowledgeable and oriented toward the technological impacts of telecommunications and computers and some of these other devices and systems that Os Ganley has talked about.

There are also, of course, groups within the Congress that have special interests that we should all be aware of. For example, the Judiciary Committees have concerns about "intellectual property rights," and the Senate Finance Committee and the House Ways and Means Committee continue to look at the so-called trade issues. But what concerns so many people both here and abroad is developing a coherent, single "information" policy, as difficult as that will be to shape.

We have heard a lot already about the role of technology, and I am not going to embellish that. I might call your attention, though, to a particularly thought-provoking book by Dr. Edward Wenk, Jr., a former mentor of mine, long on the Washington scene, who was a science adviser to Hubert Humphrey. He wrote in his book, *Margins for Survival* that "technology has locked nations together in one world." One world -- a throwback to Wendell Willkie! For with swift transportation and communication, events anywhere exert effects *everywhere*. I often think in today's world that we would do well, perhaps, to have that reminder engraved someplace, because it is terribly important.

Well, what are these leading issues? Some have been touched on already, but let me mention one or two. First of all, in the communications trade area, we have seen the United States in its general posture slip from being a large surplus nation to one where we have an indebtedness (or a deficit) of a very large sum of money. I don't have to go into that here, but we do have to find initiatives both in terms of Executive branch desire and Congressional efforts to improve our negotiating positions with people across the seas, both in the Pacific and the Atlantic regions.

We also have a number of things that are taking place in Congress that deserve higher recognition. For example, there are proposals for regional satellite systems that would be separate from INTELSAT (see Public Law 99-93). There was a Presidential Determination, No. 85-2, which stated that separate international communications satellite systems "are required in the national interests." So some initiatives have been taken, and, of course, the FCC has had continued involvement in this area. Also look at the State Department authorizations for 1986 and 1987; many of you here were more than indirectly affected. Those particular measures provided for a reaffirmation of U.S. support for INTELSAT and stated that it is U.S. policy to provide consumers with service from other satellite facilities because, to repeat myself, this would "be in the best national interests." And, in some of the supplemental appropriations, there was language that provided guidance to the FCC and the Executive branch in general for pursuing U.S. policy in this area.

Mention has also been made here about the advances that have been made in satellite systems, in fiber optics cables, and some of the other more exotic and high performance technologies. Consider that today, and this is an actual statistic, some 3,500 commercially available on-line information services exist throughout the world -- 3,500. It is enough to make most of us realize--and I'm going back to your opening comment, Mr. Ambassador -- that it is very difficult to know what is out there, much less how we find criteria by which to make these selections that allow accessing the information that is so critical to all of us.

What we have also seen in action on the Hill and in the Executive branch has been a number of proposals for organizational changes. Some of these have been spurious, but others, I believe, are very well founded. They range from the creation of a special ambassadorial group or a new interagency coordinating mechanism, to the designation of one elite agency in the Executive branch or the creation of a mechanism in the Executive Office of the President. In the meantime, as an alternative, there is always the possibility, of course, of reorganizing relevant responsibilities within the agencies -- State, Department of Commerce, USIA, and so forth.

We have a couple of other key public laws that I would like to mention in passing for the record. First, Public Law 98-164 -- this, of course, was the one that created the Office of the Coordinator for International Communications and Information Policy. Without exaggeration, this was a momentous occasion, not favorably viewed in all quarters but nonetheless a step toward having some focal location or mechanism that could carry out some of these activities. This was particularly important.

The Department of State, as you know, has been involved heavily in these matters throughout the past decade, and its charges through Congressional mandates have ranged all the way from studying scientific and technical information impacts to reporting on international communications policy. I noticed that in Public Law 100-204 in this Congress there is an authorization providing $250,000 for telecommunications development primarily for the ITU Center for Telecommunications Development. There is also a bill that has just passed both the House and the Senate. This is the Trade and International Economic Policy Reform Act. The Act declares primary U.S. negotiating objectives regarding telecommunications products and services and also looks particularly at the question of providing access to the basic telecommunications networks in foreign countries -- *foreign* countries -- on a reasonable and nondiscriminatory basis. This would allow some of our corporations and other information providers to offer what we call "value added services." For example, take a basic data base and add interpretative or analytical commentary and you have a different kind of product. These are truly important developments that have taken place.

One of my concerns, as a closing comment, is that we should be very cautious about becoming overly dependent on electronic support systems. Now, when I say this there is usually a lot of favorable lip service support but little else. The onrush, if you will, the inexorable progress being made in bringing computers and telecommunications and other devices into our lives makes this political development most difficult to comprehend or cope with. For a person who is spending a lot of time these days in "crisis management," there is logical concern about this growing over-dependence on electronic systems. Suppose we have another power blackout on the East Coast, and don't tell me this couldn't happen! When such "advanced" systems go down, what are the backups? Too often today we have committed all of our key files to an electronic form and no longer have any kind of backup. I am not suggesting that we use the stone and chisel or that we go back to the heliograph or the messenger pigeon. I am only saying that if you thoughtfully examine the kinds of support and reliance that we place in some of these vital areas, you will be as concerned as I am.

I want to conclude with a marvelous quotation from Admiral Richard Byrd, who spoke of the "cosmos of communication." Who could ignore that? He said that "the ability to transcend distance and disorder -- to reach beyond the sights and sounds of the immediate environment -- to dispatch in a universal language concepts, commentaries, and interpretations for others to share, reflect upon, and respond to "must be-- *must* be -- one of the most critical elements of our contemporary well being and our future survival.

AMBASSADOR TUTHILL: Many thanks. Would you repeat the title of Dr. Wenk's book? I'm sure a lot of people would like it.

MR. CHARTRAND: Dr. Edward Wenk published this book, *Margins for Survival*, through Pergamon Press in 1979. He is generally considered to be among the more thoughtful and certainly one of the most literate contributors to this field. His most recent book, which came out in 1986, was called *Tradeoffs: Imperatives of Choice in a High Tech World.* I would commend both books, not because of my fortunate personal association with the author,but because they are viewed so favorably by people throughout the world.

AMBASSADOR TUTHILL: Thank you. We are open for questions or comments.

QUESTION FROM THE FLOOR: What role is the Office of Technology Assessment playing?

MR. CHARTRAND: The Office of Technology Assessment (OTA) was created in 1972, as a sister agency, we in the Congressional Research Service had a small hand because we did help write the OTA charter. People like Jane Bortnick and myself work very closely on a continuing basis with OTA. As you probably know, its assignments come as a result of formal requests from one or more Congressional committees, asking in most instances that they undertake what I would call a long-term, thorough look at a given area. In many cases, Jane and I and others in our organization, plus people from the Congressional Budget Office and the House and Senate, are invited as working panel or task force members to collaborate with them and thus have the fortunate opportunity of helping perhaps to make some small contribution to selected OTA projects.

There is, for example, a major study underway at OTA called, if I can remember the marvelous title, "Technology, Public Policy and the Changing Nature of Federal Information Dissemination." Harold Relyea and I are the two CRS representatives on that particular study. So OTA does fulfill a very important role as a legislative entity that is responsive to the leadership, committees, and subcommittees of the House and Senate, and it has made some very fine contributions.

AMBASSADOR TUTHILL: I am glad you asked that question, because I have found the OTA studies to be first rate.

MR. EUGENE SCHAEFFER: May I just add that the OTA has done a very informative memo on commercial news gathering in space based on a workshop last year. It deals with the French SPOT satellite, with the political security aspects, potential First Amendment problems, etc.

AMBASSADOR TUTHILL: I support what you say about that document. I think you have to start in the back on the policy issues, and then you can work back into the technical aspects. But it's extremely interesting.

QUESTION FROM THE FLOOR: Given the diversity and the spread of the responsibility for information systems and communication policy of the U.S. government as we move into a new administration, perhaps you might speculate on how the government, based on your experience, should reorganize itself to deal with the problem of the information age in the 1990's. Should there be a lead agency? Should there be more coherence in the administrative apparatus that supports these endeavors?

MR. CHARTRAND: There would have been a time when I might have said a lead agency concept was doable. I don't think that is true now. But I think that you find two or three things happening about which we can be very optimistic. One is that the so-called role of the information resources management person or office in various agencies is gradually being strengthened and broadened. While there is still great variance among agencies, there is a general increase in appreciation for how information can best be managed and the way in which a directive from the Congress -- whether it be the creation of a clearing house or an information service or some responsibility, let's say, to an international group -- is to be carried out.

I hate to state the obvious, but we all know that success in any agency comes in many cases because of the personalities involved. I know that is a truism, but there are numerous examples that we can all cite of the key role of *the* individual, the man or woman with the strength and the political savoir faire, who understands the system and can make it work. So it seems to me that is one step that is taking place.

Secondly, I think that there is a generally higher level of sophistication, certainly in the Congress and I think elsewhere, in terms of what will be possible and how we move forward. One area, for example, that I think Congress needs to address is the strengthening once again of the Office of Science and Technology Policy for the President. Now, I certainly am not the only person saying this. William Carey, Frank Press and many, many other people have addressed this point. But if you are going to have firsthand attention paid to these issues at the highest levels in government, as we did have, for example, back in the days of John Kennedy, when

Jerry Weisner, Harvey Brooks, Ed Wenk and others were playing roles in that particular arena, then it seems to me that there is going to have to be conscious and formal attention paid to this particular area. I'm not saying that is the only magic office, but I am giving this as a readily available example.

AMBASSADOR TUTHILL: Maybe other members of our panel would like to comment on this.

DR. LEESON: I have a few observations, having been involved directly in trying to solve this problem. It's an insoluble problem, I have concluded. This is because there are numerous areas involved here, and different agencies have primary responsibility for one or another of these areas. U.S. Trade Recorder (USTR) has responsibility for trade, for example. The Federal Communications Commission has responsibility for regulatory policy, the Defense Department and the defense community for the defense aspects of communications, and so on.

Each has the upper hand in some very important aspect of the field. None are willing or, perhaps even by their mandates, able to concede authority. Their primary authority may have been given to them by Congress or by the Executive. To subordinate that authority to a central agency would be difficult or impossible. I think the best that can be done is to create an effective coordinating function, and even that is very difficult to accomplish successfully for many reasons -- because of the egos involved, because of the mandates of the agencies involved, because of the shift in the importance of issues over a period of time. I think it is too optimistic to assume that there can be a single policy and that such a policy can be administered from a single hill top.

DR. GANLEY: I am completely in agreement with what has been said. First, the topic is so broad that it covers just about every government activity that you can think of, from defense to trade to competitiveness -- so it is impossible to think that one person or one organization will handle it. Second, I think the point that Ken made is a very important one. We looked at that in our Program for a number of years. A lot of agencies have direct mandates in their enabling legislation or in later amendments. Congress becomes disgusted about one thing or another that the President has done, so it gives specific authority to a particular agency. We have found that even in the national defense area the President's authority is extremely limited, except under the most extraordinary circumstances -- let us say, an all out war, in which case all kinds of things can be overridden. But under the normal 20th century national emergency type of conditions often not even the President has authority over a particular agency. Just now, in the Trade Bill, it is being attempted to give the Trade Representative certain powers which, if I understand the final amendments, the President can override in certain circumstances. The best you can hope for is some kind of coordination. Actually, my own feeling is that this has worked remarkably well, though occasionally one gets rather frustrated.

MR. ARMISTEAD LEE: I want to ask a question about protection of intellectual property. I am sure that in the field of software and computer design there is the same phenomenon of justification of patent piracy on the part of LDCs that I have run across in the field of pharmaceutical protection. LDCs feel that they have a right to these things and that the patent system is imperialist and exploitative, and so on. Is any progress being made within the framework of the GATT and elsewhere to win over these professional pirate countries?

AMBASSADOR TUTHILL: Anyone volunteer to answer this one?

DR. GANLEY: I would start out with the general observation that until shortly after World War I the United States was the greatest pirate nation in the world. We stole just about anything that came to mind, from chemical processes to books, to copyrights. And then it became to our commercial advantage to change. It is very definitely to the United States' commercial advantage, in the age of information that we are talking about today, to try to enforce intellectual property rights very vigorously.

I think some progress is being made, both by bilateral pressure and through actions in the World Intellectual Property Organization (WIPO). It is a subject now in the GATT negotiations on services, but I think progress will be slow. Probably one thing that will help more than anything else, at least in certain industrial areas, is that the corporations, rather than the government, will say, well, we are not going to transfer certain types of sensitive technologies to you unless we are assured that you can protect them. After a while that starts to sink in.

But, of course, we are talking not just about industrial types of things. We are talking about records, about videos. I think it will be very difficult, and with the new technologies, particularly the VCR technology, it will be just about impossible.

AMBASSADOR TUTHILL: One more question. Karl?

MR. KARL MAUTNER: This is really a technical question. Isn't the geosynchronous orbit getting awfully crowded?

DR. LEESON: Yes, it's getting crowded in certain senses, though I frankly am a little bit out of touch with how crowded it is today. When I left the issue three years ago there was concern that it was getting more crowded by the day. There have, however, been some technological fixes in the sense of changing satellite spacing policy. The Federal Communications Commission, for example, in the U.S. permits closer spacing, which permits the packing of more satellites in a given amount of satellite orbital space. The problem of crowding may well be assuaged o some extent by the growth of an alternative technology -- fiber optics. This technology provides a very high capacity, high speed, inexpensive way of moving vast amounts of information over large geographic areas which will take some of the pressure off of satellite traffic. Those are my observations.

AMBASSADOR TUTHILL: Thank you very much. We thank the three members of the panel very much for a very interesting presentation.

II

IPLICATIONS FOR AMERICAN FOREIGN POLICY AND DIPLOMACY

II

TOPIC I: COMMUNICATIONS ISSUES
DIANA LADY DOUGAN, former Coordinator for International Communications and Information Policy Department of State; Presently, Senior advisor and Chair, International Communications, CSIS
WILLIAM C. SALMON, Executive Officer, National Academy of Engineering

TOPIC II: ECONOMIC ISSUES
ROBERT J. SAMUELSON, Columnist on Economics and Business, *Newsweek* and *Washington Post*
RICHARD D. KAUZLARICH, Deputy Director for Economics, Policy Planning Staff, Department of State

TOPIC III: POLITICAL AND SECURITY ISSUES
WALTER RAYMOND, JR., Assistant Director U. S. Information Agency

AMBASSADOR TUTHILL: We will start, with your permission, with Ambassador Dougan, who was until very recently the State Department's Coordinator for International Communications and Information Policy.

I: COMMUNICATIONS ISSUES

AMBASSADOR DIANA LADY DOUGAN: During my five plus years as the first U.S. Coordinator for International Communications and Information Policy, I spent considerable time doing missionary work in gaining converts to the idea that communications and information issues should be considered an important priority in our foreign policy.

Within a year after I came on board, the position of U.S. Coordinator and the logic of locating it in the State Department gained the formal statutory support of Congress. However as a practical matter it was much more difficult to get the bureaucratic

27

and institutional resources committed in the State Department. Although we were successful in establishing a formal Bureau in the Department to support the Coordinator function, it was not an easy concept to sell in the tradition-coated halls of State. Thus I'm especially pleased to see a conference such as this which accepts as a premise that communications and information policy issues have become essential ingredients in the conduct of foreign policy.

As a starting point, it is essential to keep in mind that the U.S. has historically viewed the ownership and operation of the electronic means of communication as basically non-governmental functions. By contrast, most of the world has viewed the control of the airwaves and conduits of communications as vital functions of government. Indeed, even countries who share our commitment to the free flow of information have felt that the conduits of communications are too important politically, economically and strategically to leave in the hands of the private sectors. Telephone systems as well as radio and television stations have generally evolved under direct governmental supervision. With the explosion of telecommunications technology and its increased affordability and accessibility on a global basis the policies and operations in virtually all countries are starting to change.

In my role as U.S. Coordinator, I was responsible not only for overseeing the policy interests involving over fourteen federal agencies. Equally challenging was trying to make sense and cohesive policy initiatives out of the diverse and competing private sector interests.

As foreign service officers, you have had to deal with the realities of government ownership of the telephone systems as well as the radio and television stations. The impacts of foreign ownership of the media is readily understood in the foreign policy community. Indeed the delivery and interpretation of information is the stock in trade of diplomacy. Foreign governments' use of the airwaves to package and promote the goals of the administration in power have long been considered an important political equation. What has been less understood and only recently acknowledged is the increasingly important role that electronic communications plays in economic and strategic terms.

For example, in terms of international trade, America's third largest area of export is now represented by communications equipment and services. In the broader economic context, the sudden affordability and accessibility of international transmission of data has become the driving force in international commerce. In the process, the telecommunications regulatory policies and practices of other countries and the decisions of the International Telecommunications Union directly impact on the ability of virtually any American company to function abroad.

In strategic terms, the U.S. has a considerable national security stake in communications issues. For example, the U.S. military is the world's single largest user of international telecommunications services. That's not counting the Defense communities own networks of milsats and other dedicated communications systems.

Communications issues are clearly not just technical issues for engineers and scientists, but rather a complicated blend of economic, political and strategic interests. In that context, I must candidly say that one of my initial surprises when I first came to the State Department was to discover that more often than not other federal agencies have come to view the State Department as a sort of incidental translator -- a bureaucratic and foreign language translator. Too often I believe the Department, especially in areas involving technology, are inclined to defer to the parochial interests of other agencies rather than take on what I believe is their proper coordinating leadership role of sorting out the balance of political, economic and strategic interests which make for good policy.

By way of background, when the Office of Telecommunications Policy was disbanded under the Carter Administration, its functions were spread all over the federal government, but most particularly the Commerce Department with the establishment of the National Telecommunications and Information Agency (NTIA). In the process, the State Department was given the lead on international communications policy issues, but there was frankly little appreciation for what those issues were or how important they had become. When I was approached by the Reagan Administration to take on the responsibility of being the first U.S. Coordinator for International Communications and Information Policy, the White House almost forgot to mention that the position was located in the State Department.

I recall early in my tenure having a very pleasant private lunch with then Secretary of Commerce Baldridge. We talked at length about the many emerging issues and challenges that the U.S. was facing internationally and the importance the field had to American foreign policy. But at the end of lunch, he said in essence, "You know, Diana, you really belong over here, because basically communications is a trade issue." While on the one hand I appreciated the fact that a cabinet office was taking time and understood that this was an important issue, I also had to say politely that our government was at least attempting to see this as an issue that went beyond trade, beyond strategic or geopolitical considerations and for that reason, I was asked to provide that focal point in the State Department, not the Commerce or Defense Department.

I would like now to offer a few thoughts that may serve as a basis to provoke some of your morning's discussion.

As I mentioned, I see this area as one that involves a balance of foreign policy issues. At our peril do we look at them in isolation as technical issues or economic issues or political issues or strategic issues. I have found Foreign Service officers in general very intimidated by technology. I think the foreign policy community has been in large measure intimidated by it and therefore not particularly well equipped to deal with it.

There are several points that I would like to cover briefly regarding communications issues that I hope will at least give you a taste of some of the broad concerns and how they are interrelated. One obviously has to do with the growing availability and accessibility of communications, which the first panel has covered in rather sparkling detail. There is now an ability to communicate, to reach out and be affordable to individuals even in the farthest corners of the world.

What does that mean? It means that nations are bypassed, that sovereignty is bypassed. So I would suggest to you that the communications policy area first of all is playing havoc with the whole concept of sovereignty. When you think about the ownership and control of information as a basis of sovereignty, the movement of currency, the movement of goods, these are things that historically have been very much at the core of government controls.

When we read the book, 1984, I think we were seized with the fear that communications technology was going to become a more centralizing force. "Big brother" was going to exercise centralized control. I think for a variety of reasons, which will be discussed by subsequent panels, that information technology is having the opposite effect. It is becoming a very decentralizing force, and ultimately there is more control in the hands of individuals. So as we look into foreign policy in the 21st century, I think we will see a world that is going to have to deal with very different and substantially increased numbers of players, both as individuals and as countries.

This brings me to my second point, which concerns the Third World. In my view, we are seeing a world in which the newly industrialized countries and the industrialized countries are becoming more of a grouping. The real question relates to the vastly underdeveloped countries. But there is an opportunity for the underdeveloped countries to become not Luddites but participants in the use of communications technology. Global electronic communication substantially offset the tyranny of geography, the lack of natural resources and many of the other things that have plagued many of these countries. One cannot ignore histories, cultures and traditions, but there is nevertheless going to be an increased homogenization of the world even in the least developed countries.

When you think, for example, that there were more color television sets sold in China last year than in the whole rest of the world combined, that gives you a sense of some of the changing dynamics.

Consider a factory in Mauritius that makes sweaters for The Limited Company. Now, instead of producing one sweater in one pattern and one color, the factory can today, through computer design and management, do overnight change orders and can provide the whole new fashion range of what 7th Avenue in New York wants. When you consider the data links that are encircling the world, you start focusing on what even a limited but educated work force can do regardless of location.

You may have read recently in the newspaper that United Airlines is bailing itself out by selling a substantial interest in its computer reservation services, and it is also selling to foreign partners. (I might add that American Airlines is making more net profit on its computer reservation service than it is on its airplane business.) United has just gone into a partnership with airlines from other countries. Most of these airlines do the actual processing and computing in the Caribbean, not in the United States.

My third point is that our foreign policy challenge with the developing countries is to make them recognize that they are players, that they have a stake in technology. Unfortunately, too often, technical forums become political forums -- especially if some of the countries involved don't recognize they have a positive stake in the technical decisions. When I first came to the State Department the International Telecommunications Union (ITU) was practically ready for self destruction because of the whole issue of the expulsion of Israel. What that had to do with telecommunications is anybody's guess. At the same time we were also faced with heavy media politics in UNESCO. And a lot of people were lumping those two organizations together as ones that were overly politicized and of less and less use to the United States.

You know what our decision was on UNESCO, but with the ITU we took the opposite tack. We took the position that it served U.S. interests and that even those most opposed to multilateral organizations would have to recognize that the ITU was not simply a necessary evil, but a necessary good for bringing order to the radio spectrum, to standards and to the other issues that literally make communication across borders successful in developing as well as developed countries.

I think it is noteworthy that five and a half years later, having started from the position of seriously doubting whether we should continue to stay in the ITU organization, we now have a situation where it is one of only two multilateral organizations that the United States supports on all criteria -- NATO being the other. And part of the reason for that, I think, has been not only our own increased attention to the organization and willingness to be constructive and positive, but our considerable success in helping the Third World to realize that whether it is a matter of the geostationary orbit or the radio spectrum they should not hold it hostage for political reasons, because they too can benefit from it.

Two additional points I want to touch on in the foreign policy context are the European community and NATO. The European Community for many Americans is a sort of mixed blessing, because while we support the Community in the context of the Treaty of Rome and its breaking down of barriers, we also have a growing concern, especially regarding telecommunications, that Pan-Europeanism has some potentially negative, protectionist aspects. Last year the European Community formally staked out a claim to make telecommunications an area of competency.

Initially I think a lot of people were very dismissive of the EC's initiative. They felt the PTTs would never let go, and again this was an area that had much to do with sovereignty. But when the EC found that it was butting its head against the institutional walls of individual countries, instead of trying to beat the PTTs it co-opted them and reinforced their role. The European Community's so-called green paper on telecommunications, from a U.S. perspective, is something of a mixed bag. It is probably more positive than negative, because the emphasis is on opening up markets, but a lot of the emphasis is also on putting power and strength back into the PTTs and at a time when more and more European countries are considering privatization and competition. Why do we have a problem? Because this reinforces government ownership and control and monopoly approaches to the deliverers of communications. We think not only that this is not in the United States interest, it is not in the interest of reinforcing a robust global economy.

Let me turn now to the NATO Alliance. When you think about the changing dynamics of the Alliance and the increased pressure, particularly here in the United States, for the Europeans in so-called "burden-sharing," I think we must be increasingly mindful of the relationships between our NATO commitment to defense and the European Community commitment to make telecommunications a high trade priority. For example, the EC has established the European Telecommunications Standards Institute to develop European standards. During its organizational stages we have been pushing at the door to make sure that U.S. companies and U.S. interests can participate in this process. But if we are faced with a world where European standards in a high percentage of technology -- and telecommunications represents a high percentage of defense technology -- are different from those of the United States or if we have more confrontation between the economic goals of the

European community and the strategic goals of the NATO Alliance, I think we are going to have some real problems down the pike. We have been very complacent over the years about U.S. standards and technology, particularly telecommunications technology. Until its breakup, AT&T in many respects represented U.S. interests directly as the standard bearer in many telecommunications issues. And the United States was also acting as essentially the unilateral leader of NATO. Today, this is no longer the case so we'd better keep an eye on the consequences of these substantially changed dynamics, especially when economic aggression is gaining equal footing with military aggression as a policy priority.

Finally, I would like to comment on the increasingly blurred lines between domestic and foreign policy when it comes to communications issues. At what point is something a domestic policy and at what point is it an international policy? That determination and sorting out may be our biggest challenge of the future, especially as we have become a service economy. Sixty-three percent of the U.S. labor force now works in the service sector, not in manufacturing. That service sector is, if not totally dependent, highly dependent on telecommunications to work and to function.

In the communications field in the past, because we are a large country, whether the issue related to standards, tariffs, the spectrum allocation, or general regulatory practices we could make and enforce decisions in almost splendid isolation. We can no longer do that. We have become dependent on other countries, and we serve other countries as a service economy. So increasingly we have to find means and mechanisms to make the synapse between domestic and international policy. The more we attempt to deregulate and liberalize communications policy domestically, the more we must overcome traditions and contradictions abroad. I might add that fewer and fewer issues fall inside the traditional foreign policy compasses of North-South or East-West relations. Communications technology is essentially insensitive to geography and geopolitics. It is essential that the foreign policy professionals understand the growing impact of information technology if they are to effectively orchestrate much less coordinate foreign policy.

AMBASSADOR TUTHILL: Thank you very much. We now turn to Mr. William Salmon, who is Executive Officer of the National Academy of Engineering and formerly a Foreign Service officer.

WILLIAM C. SALMON: Thank you. My comments here will be based on my experience in the Department of State, rather than my present activities in the Academy of Engineering.

Historical change, according to Marshall McLuhan, has been caused principally by changes in the dominant medium of communication. He divided human history into three parts: before the printing press, after Gutenberg, and the electronic or information age. The convergence and continuing advancement of computer and communication technologies are moving us inevitably towards his global village.

I would like to expand briefly on that and to look in a little more detail at some history, to look at new technologies as they come on the scene and see how those technologies contribute to changes in people and how they do things. From my point of view, information and the ability to communicate have no value per se. Rather, it is what the individual will do with the information once he has it. It is what the individual will do when he can communicate. And it is what others will do when they have confidence that someone has information or an ability to communicate.

One of the things that I have tried to do, but have never really had time to do, is to develop a graph, covering 20 centuries on the horizontal scale. On the vertical scale we would chart units of communication activity. The value on the vertical scale 20 centuries ago would be close to zero. As we proceed through the centuries toward the present, the value increases with the travel of people and the growth in population, and the slope noticeably increases with printing. But with today's technology the graph goes off the chart as we approach the present time. Technologies have contributed to that growth in communication. Communication, in this sense, is one person "talking" to another, conveying a message in any form that communicates ideas among people. Today's revolution, or evolution, in technologies has brought tremendous volumes of communication. That is what we need to keep in mind.

An interesting historical point that I was told of years ago is that the development of the stirrup permitted farmers to go a little farther afield from their homes and thus contributed to larger collections of people, helping to lay the groundwork for the growth of cities.

Communications are a necessary ingredient in the development of our society, in how we get along with each other and in our standard of living.

I would like to look on today's abilities in communications as also determining how our society will develop. Distance is no longer a factor in communications. It remains a factor in the movement of raw materials, but as others have noted, the economy that we enjoy today is more and more determined by the movement of information, relatively speaking, and less and less by the movement of physical goods.

As I look at the effects of today's communications and related technologies, I think the most significant consequence of the applications of modern technologies will be to change the ways people relate to their governments, the way people in one country relate to those in other countries, and the way governments relate to one another publicly.

The United States is perhaps the world's most open society, and we are undergoing significant changes due to modern communication technologies. In some Western societies there is perhaps a little less openness, and it is my belief that they will undergo more significant changes than we will. At the other end of this spectrum of openness, are the Eastern European countries and the Soviet Union. We are already seeing very significant changes in the USSR. That society will undergo even more change than we over this period of time as advanced communications technologies are put into operation and people use them.

There is a question as to whether these technologies can be used by governments to control more efficiently the information their people have, or whether individuals will be able to use them to gain more information than governments wish them to have. In the short term, there are many opportunities for a government, usually having more resources than individuals, to contain, control, and limit information. It is my belief, however, that in the long run the application of today's technologies and innovations will give the individual the opportunity to get more information. The individual will win out in the long term. Opportunities for people to have more information will produce changes in governments. People become more democratic as they are better informed.

Now, in looking at today's technologies -- I don't mean to stick with the stirrup -- let's focus on modern communications and information technologies -- satellites and fiber optics. What is the general direction of change in these technologies, and how will this change influence what people do, how they use them? The general trend is one of continuous decline in the cost of information transfer. How much of a decline and how rapidly, I am not certain, but in simple terminology each individual with a computer can have at his desk top all the static information that he might want. He may have too much. He may not have an ability to control it all and to use it wisely, but the technology to permit him to have great quantities of information will be there.

The central computer is a storage place for what I call non-static information. What is the latest price of a stock sold on the New York Stock Exchange? That would be in a central computer of some form. What happened to a stock yesterday and in years past can be brought to your desk. Adding other sources and types of information, you will get a sense of what I see as the effects of the decline in the cost of the transfer of information as well as our ability to store larger and larger quantities of information in personal computers.

We will increase the reliability of our technology and our equipment, as well as our ability to handle these large amounts of information. We are not going to become completely error free. We may still face the threat of an East Coast blackout, for example, but I think we will reduce the probability of that significantly.

We talked a bit here about terrestrial versus space based communications. The capability of fiber optics to connect any land based points for information transfer leaves satellite communications systems to serve mobile communications and connections with remote areas.

The policies that we have been pursuing should still be pursued. Promoting the free flow of information does not mean news without cost. It means there should be no established limitations on the flow of information that are not justified by the health of the society. We do not permit people to yell fire in a theatre. We have national security controls. But the presumption should be in favor of free flow among peoples. A corollary to that, is that there should be a presumption that the right to control that information flow, to have it go from point A and be received at point B, rests with the individual and not with the government. A challenge that should at the top of the list for American foreign policy in the general area of communications is to see that the principle of the free flow of information is practiced in all activities we engage in with other countries in helping them to establish communication systems and in the policies we pursue in UNESCO, the U.N. and any other international body.

I was pleased to hear the new Secretary General of UNESCO talk about his interest in communications. The constitution of UNESCO includes the right of individuals to have access to information. I wish him well in applying this portion of his mandate. We as a nation must pursue the principle of free flow of information as our main foreign policy objective in the communications area.

Thank you.

AMBASSADOR MILTON BARALL: From Ambassador Dougan we have heard about disagreements in the government and how difficult it is for the State Department to exercise leadership. And from Mr. Salmon we have heard about the bewildering problems resulting from the enormous explosion of technology in the world. The question is how does all this affect the ability of the United States to conduct any diplomatic policy. I am interested in the role of an embassy and the role of the State Department in exercising leadership. Is it impossible?

AMBASSADOR DOUGAN: You may have answered your question. I think a later segment of the discussion will deal more specifically with this, but you do raise a point that concerns not just embassies. It concerns businesses competitive advantage, security. It goes to all areas. The presumed increase in access means that the other guy is going to have the same information you have. But as Bill Salmon pointed out, part of the problem is what you do with the information.

I think the role of embassies has eroded in many respects for many reasons. The fact that it is too easy and too inviting to bypass the embassy has changed substantially the decision-making process as well as the information gathering and analysis process. I believe this also would suggest that the State Department itself has to change a bit. Its biggest resource has always been people, and the ability to bring more sophistication to the analysis, not being the single caretaker of the analysis. This maybe where the State Department and the Foreign Service have had the hardest period of adjustment. They are no longer the caretakers of information and analysis in the way they have been historically.

And so what do they have to be? They have to be better analyzers, better extrapolators, better message carriers, and there has to be an increased level of sophistication for that true diplomatic role. It is very humbling to see how people in industry and people in other agencies have much more information in many instances than the State Department itself has. It has been very slow to get its own technological act together.

One of the things that came out of our workshop last fall at the National Academy of Sciences, which we put together for the Secretary of State, was that one of the problems with the State Department and one of the reasons they will always have difficulty in recognizing the importance of this policy area is that they themselves are computer illiterate. They are technologically illiterate.

I remember being in some bilateral discussions at The Hague a few months back, when Ambassador John Shad, a former chairman of the Securities and Exchange Commission, told me about a wrestling match within the embassy in which the Luddites prevailed. They decided they did not want a fax machine in the embassy to insure instant communication with the U.S. because it would undercut the traditional cabled messages. So what did the more impatient officials do? They went to a local brokerage house and used their fax machines.

AMBASSADOR TUTHILL: Do you want to comment on that?

MR. SALMON: Yes, please. Change, yes. Loss of leadership, no. I think that the nature of the responsibilities of an ambassador over the past 300 years has changed as communications have increased. That change will continue. You will never find a status quo, but the ability of the ambassador to lead the American mission in a country should not change in any way. We find criticism today of how fast changes in technologies are being absorbed, used and applied. But I don't sense that there is any need for the leadership quality to change. As a department, we have got to stay up with what the technology has to offer, understand it, apply it, take advantage of it to meet the responsibilities of the Department, including the embassy. I sense no need for a lack of leadership.

AMBASSADOR TUTHILL: Just one more question.

MR. DAVID BURNS: The words "free flow" have been used, and people have also alluded to the cost. I think it is important to note that free flow of information does not mean inexpensive information. Given the fact that there is a fire hose of information, it is very difficult to get an individual drink of water from a fire hose. And the value added guys are the ones who are able to filter or to control the flow so that the individual can get what he needs when he wants it. But that is not cheap. Anybody who has a teenager with a modem and a telephone and a computer in his house is startled at how quickly the bill can run up. And I have had personal experience in being seduced by information vendors and finding that I simply cannot afford to get the information that they could supply. So I really do want to draw attention to the distinction between flow, which is enormous, and the cost, even the cost of the individual controlling or accessing the flow.

Secondly, I would like to draw attention to a distinction between communication and understanding. I think all of us have had experiences in which communication provides opportunities and rapid possibility for misunderstanding.

MR. SALMON: These are exactly the points I was making. I want the company that wishes to sell you a piece of processed information to be free to sell you that information. I want you to be free to accept it. The cost is another factor, another dimension. And what you do with information, whether it goes in one ear or out the other or some of it is retained, is another factor.

AMBASSADOR TUTHILL: Do you want to comment on this, Ambassador Dougan?

AMBASSADOR DOUGAN: Although the points are all valid, keep in mind that with the increased pace of technology things are getting faster, smaller and cheaper. And so notwithstanding what may be a cost, when you look at all the academic networks that are used so widely you find that very few of them pay their bills. The truth of the matter is that despite all the legitimate institutionally framed bases of information, there is an absolute hemorrhage of those networks because those who want to can access them. Someone earlier mentioned the fact that you can now make satellite dishes out of aluminum foil and chicken wire. This is just one of many current examples of the ability to access information, whether it is through piracy or legitimate means, is still going to get into the range of the affordable for the individual as opposed to the institution. Nothing is free, and free flow is perhaps a romantic overstatement, but the freedom of choice of being able to access information is increasing. Anyway you examine it, the art of diplomacy is being made more complex by the science of information technology.

AMBASSADOR TUTHILL: Before we go on to the next section, I really can't resist a comment about the State Department and our missions abroad. Part of the responsibility -- and I have testified before the Senate Foreign Relations Committee on this--rests with the Senate Foreign Relations Committee, which does not take seriously its role of examining ambassadorial appointees who require the "advice and consent" of the United States Senate. And in this room there are any number of people who have been up before the Senate Foreign Relations Committee. There have been many superficial and irrelevant discussions during those hearings. I'm talking about both political appointees and career officers. It often reflects an irresponsible attitude on the part of the Senate, apparently on the assumption that if the White House -- Democrats or Republicans -- wants X, why just let it go through. And this has meant putting both career and political appointees in place as ambassadors who are not competent to do the job.

Let's go on to the next section.

AMBASSADOR TUTHILL: Our first panelist in this section of our discussion is Mr. Robert J. Samuelson, syndicated columnist. His name is familiar to anyone who reads *Newsweek* or the *Washington Post*.

II: ECONOMIC ISSUES

ROBERT J. SAMUELSON: I will try to be as brief as possible, in part because others have already covered the ideas that I thought were going to be original to me.

Speaking about the economic effects of communications, let me point out four basic trends which I think are related to each other. The first, mentioned by Ambassador Dougan, is the trend towards decentralization and deconcentration of economic power. This has really been going on since the 19th century, but it has accelerated enormously since the end of the Second World War. We are not just talking about microprocessors, but about telephone communication, about cheaper jet travel. There is really a continuum here, and computers and microprocessors are just the latest step in this evolution.

These developments give businesses an opportunity to pick and chose areas of the world where they want to locate various functions, whether it be manufacturing, trading or issuing securities, or making loans. Lower transaction costs reflecting lower communications and travel costs have opened up enormous opportunities for business to be mobile.

The second point is that this evolution has inevitably reduced the power of governments. Once enterprises can decide between different national locations for various activities and once these various activities do in fact locate around the world in different places, the power of governments to influence companies or to influence particular types of economic activity diminishes. Governments can try to offset that by coordinating among themselves, exchanging information and setting up common ground rules, but there are inherent conflicts. Governments are in a conflict of interest with themselves. They may have national and economic interests to pursue which are at odds with shared information or common ground rules for governing various sorts of activities. So it seems to me you get a reduction of political power at the expense of market power.

The third point, which tends to follow from this, is that we no longer have an adequate economic model to explain the world. It seems to me, if you go back 15 or 20 years, people in general and economists in particular, or at least American economists in particular, tended to think about the economy in the following terms:

that we had essentially a self-contained national economy, which had an international sector.

That is to say, the international sector consisted primarily of exports and imports and a few other things like tourism and royalties. But essentially our economy was a national economy, self-contained. The things that went on in the economy were primarily influenced by things that we did here in the United States, and the effects of international events upon our imports and exports were really of a second order.

This provided, in policy terms, a fairly understandable framework in which you could attempt to manipulate the economy through various policy instruments, like budget or monetary policy, interest rates or tax policies. To a lesser extent other countries had a similar model in mind. I say to a lesser extent, because European countries and even Japan have always been more conscious of their interdependence with the rest of the world than we have. But even so, I think that other countries still believed in this basic sort of model.

Now, I don't say that this model has been destroyed entirely, but it seems to be fairly apparent to everyone that we are now part of a larger global economy. I will illustrate what this means by way of analogy. Even 15 or 20 years ago no one would have presumed to describe the economy of the state of Connecticut as self-contained. You might be able to describe the economy of Connecticut in terms of employment and industrial patterns, and even growth and income levels, by a few conveniently available statistics. But no one would have said that what goes on in Connecticut is determined simply by what people in Connecticut do. People would have recognized that Connecticut is part of a larger regional or national economy.

In the same way, our economy is now part of a larger global system, but we don't understand well how this larger system operates. One anecdote underlines the extent of our ignorance. The Brookings Institution recently published a two-volume set of studies comparing all the economic models that attempt to explain how the world economy works. Although I am not an economist and don't pretend to understand how the models work in detail, if you look at the results these models generate when they are given similar sets of inputs -- they are given similar assumptions about a starting point and asked what would happen over a period of two or three years -- they do not generate the same results.

The second point is that one of the major areas by which national economies are connected with each other and by which economic forces are transmitted around the world is exchange rates. Almost every economist who is in the least bit honest about it admits that economists do not understand any longer how exchange rates are set. We may come to a better understanding in four, five or ten years, but right now there is a high level of ignorance.

The third point about what these models showed, and showed fairly consistently, to indicate the extent of the confusion that exists, is that you could simulate equivalent economic policies in the United States and the rest of the industrial world, meaning primarily Europe and Japan, and get asymmetrical results. By which I mean, if you had a tax cut or spending increase in the United States, the models would attempt to calculate the effect on the rest of the world. Then they would simulate a tax cut or a spending increase in the rest of the world to see what the effect would be on the United States.

In these models, when the United States increased spending or cut taxes, the stimulus effect on the rest of the world was greater than when the other countries cut taxes or increased spending. That, in my view, in a very elementary way reflects the historic importance of the United States as the centerpiece of the world economy in the last 40 years. But I think it also shows that we really don't know what is going on.

My last point is that we are handling these issues mainly on an ad-hoc basis. I am sure this will come as no surprise to anybody. You find ad-hoc coordination and consultation in a variety of areas, from exchange rates to bank capital to securities markets. I am sure that people who study this will deplore the fact that everything is so fragmented, but in my view this is probably the best that is available and so far it doesn't seem to be all that bad.

AMBASSADOR TUTHILL: Thank you very much. I want to add a little footnote in terms of our emphasis on internal matters. The *New York Times* recently had a long article on program trading and the inability to handle its effect on the markets. The entire article concentrated only on the United States. There was not a paragraph in that article on the fact that people all around the world are doing this as well.

The next participant is Richard Kauzlarich, who is the Deputy Director for Economics in the Policy Planning Staff in the Department of State.

RICHARD D. KAUZLARICH: Thank you, Mr. Ambassador. At this point in the program, as Bob Samuelson indicated, it becomes hard to say much that is new. I am tempted after hearing the discussion thus far to talk about things other than economics, because there are a number of issues that have been raised institutionally as well as otherwise that I would really like to get into. But let me pick up on a point that Bob made, because it is an important one.

Whatever the information age means, it does not just mean issues relating to telecommunications and information policy. You may disagree with me, Ambassador Dougan, but the danger in the State Department is not that we fail to give enough attention to telecommunications and information policy issues, but that we fail to integrate them back into our overall conduct of international economic policy. Obviously this feeds into political and security questions. So that is my introduction to this subject.

As I was preparing for this session, one of my colleagues suggested that I look at an article by De Anne Julius, a U.K. national who worked at the World Bank. It appeared in *International Affairs* in the summer of 1987 and deals with Britain's international interests in the world. I thought this article was really quite striking, because it applies as much to the United States as it does the U.K. I would like to read one section.

Ms. Julius said: "The world economy is currently undergoing structural changes whose domestic economic impact is not yet widely recognized in Britain. Outdated attitudes that focus on industrial decline and losses of historical market share in certain export categories carry with them the risk that important new opportunities for an effective British foreign economic policy will be missed. If Britain's economic interests in this changing environment are to be identified, the traditional view of economic links with the rest of the world will need to be broadened and the public debate on the new options available become better informed."

I think that is precisely the problem we face in the United States today. We really have to clarify the relationship between our position in the global economy and our role as a super power. And I am afraid that the public debate that has surrounded the Trade Bill, in particular, has not really come to grips with those issues.

Ms. Julius goes on to make a very important point for foreign policy makers. She writes: "The implicit assumptions of foreign policy makers about their country's role in the world economy and its external economic interests have an important but largely unexamined bearing on the political choices that are made." So if we assume that we are simply a national economy with a small international sector, we are going to make decisions as foreign policy makers that are not consistent with the world we operate in.

What I would like to do here is to consider some technological changes which go beyond information and telecommunications policy, but which obviously are at the heart of it, and their possible foreign policy impact. Some of these I am sure are quite familiar. Anyone reading the press and journal articles will have seen all of these before. But what I hope to add to them is perhaps a sense of reference to what this means for U.S. foreign policy. In other words, why should we be concerned about these technological changes?

First, consider developments that affect markets for raw materials. We talk a lot about fiber optics being substituted for copper wiring in the telecommunications area. That is one aspect of it, but there are technological developments that are in essence increasing the supply of existing materials and commodities. Look at developments in the aluminum industry such as the use of scrap, which accounts for 27 percent of the total consumption of aluminum in the United States. Here is an area where the basic elements that go into aluminum become less and less important as the recycling goes on.

Synthetic materials are another aspect -- and here the fiber optics issue comes most clearly into focus. The composites and other high tech materials that are being developed today will be important products tomorrow. One estimate is that by the year 2000, 32 percent of the total weight of an average automobile in the United States will consist of these high tech materials. And there is also the downsizing and miniaturization we talked about.

What is the foreign policy implication of this? It affects our attitude toward countries like Zaire and South Africa and Chile, where we may have a relationship that today is based in part on access to certain raw materials. It affects our attitude to things like The Common Funds and other ideas for commodity price stabilization. Is that a winning proposition in this new era?

Second is the question we have danced around this morning: the globalization of manufacturing. To multi-national sources of production and marketing add the idea of flexible manufacturing systems, new technologies plus the reduction in time and the costs of interactions, and the meaning of foreign and domestic entities becomes blurred. In textiles, for example, it may be just as easy to procure from Mauritius as it is to go to California. But it does bring into focus these interrelationships among government policies on exchange rates, on trade, on legal and regulatory and environmental policies. All of these so-called national issues have a very great international impact on trade and investment flows.

Now, if we fail to understand this globalization phenomenon and its impact on trade, we are going to follow misguided policies. We have a policy base in the trade area that centers on retaliation and that is vulnerable to pressure from various interest groups. Such a policy simply doesn't reflect the trends in globalization that are going on today. The semiconductor pact with Japan is an example of the problems that arise when we don't recognize the changes taking place. I think that was not a very smart move, because it is not clear in the case of semiconductors what the national interest is. There are as many interests; i.e. importers of semiconductors -- harmed by what we did as were helped by it.

Such a policy approach shifts the value that we place on imports versus exports. We have acted historically as if exports were good and imports were bad. It is not entirely clear you can make that sort of judgment today when 80 percent of U.S. firms depend on imported inputs for some aspect of their manufacturing.

The third area to consider is rapid product development and technological applications. Some companies move from being non-competitors to competitors simply because they have cut their product development time. The *Financial Times* about a year ago used the example of Xerox, which cut its development time for products from six to about three years. They were able to make a comeback from what many had regarded as disaster because they understood that the effectiveness of the process of refining a product concept is as important as how the product is made. And here you get away from technology and more into human and organizational questions that really need to be tackled. The explosion of technology around the world makes it difficult for manufacturers to maintain a lead for long as the spread of technology takes place.

In this environment can a government in fact pick a winner in a high tech race with the technology evolving as rapidly as it is? And in the area of intellectual property, mentioned earlier, it does raise certain questions about what sort of protection we do have in our intellectual property policy when countries and companies can use rapid product evolution essentially as a competitive tool in the same way patents were used in the past.

Fourth is globalization of financial markets. We are seeing financial markets of a trillion dollars a day. That is more than the federal budget of the United States for one year. These flows are not just reflections of movements in our own current account, as we economists have been taught. They move on their own and are economic forces in their own right. When our holdings or holdings of other countries become so large -- whether they are loans or direct investment or portfolio investment -- they can have a major influence on our external position.

Deregulation of financial markets has been a boon, but as was pointed out in the little article on program trading, there are downsides to that. A whole new set of financial instruments and off-balance-sheet activities may require international attention. It makes you wonder whether we have reached the limits of macroeconomic coordination when you are dealing with problems of this nature.

Finally on the services side, I would take exception to describing the U.S. economy as a service economy. I think if you look at the percentage of GNP represented by manufacturing output over the years, it has been relatively stable. In the employment sector, however, service employment has really shot up. The goods and services interrelationship has become more tightly developed. *Scientific American,* in a study of high technology in the services industry a few months ago, reported that for the average manufacturer about 75 to 85 percent of his value added comes from the services side. So what I think we are seeing is a bundling of goods and services in ways in which we are not used to seeing them. In a way, that calls into question trying to focus exclusively on services as a separate item within the GATT.

What do all of these isolated, apparently independent technological developments mean? As Bob Samuelson pointed out, we are not an isolated national economy. What is national and what is foreign is not clear. This fact carries with it some fairly significant political impacts. It suggests something that I think it is worth considering: how nations will relate to each other in groups or individually as a result of these technological changes. As we have thought about these relationships, the problem for everyone, whether it is the United States or Chad, is that somehow we have to become or remain competitive in an environment that is very different.

It seems to us that there are going to be three categories of countries emerging in this information age. These will become very important for the way we conduct our foreign policy. First, we will have the obvious leading edge countries who are innovators and absorbers of these technological changes and benefit from them in the broadest economic sense. Most of them will be large countries -- the U.S., Japan, the European countries. Some may be small. Some may be newly industrialized countries (NICs) today or may even be developing countries that will grow in the future. A second group will simply be absorbers of technology. Although they may have technological capability, they simply are not at the stage in the evolution of their social and economic structures that allows them to become serious innovators of new technology. This need not be a permanent condition, but there are countries that are going to be in the catch-up stage for a good long while.

Finally, there are the countries that we ought to be most concerned about from a foreign policy point of view: the marginal participants. Not all of these countries will be poor by any means. You are likely to find some fairly wealthy countries that simply are unable to participate either as significant absorbers or innovators in this information age. A number of these countries will then become fair game for political and other sorts of instability. They have to be thought of as a group that requires some particular foreign policy attention in an era where GNP alone is not going to determine whether or not countries are successful and where some of the changes that have to take place are ones that really have to come on the internal side of many of these economies.

AMBASSADOR TUTHILL: Let me congratulate both of the speakers on the fact that they avoided the words which were so commonly used in the Kennedy years of Walter Heller and Jim Tobin and Bob Solow and Bob Rosa, namely, "fine tuning" of the economy. I'm glad those words aren't used anymore. But we believed it then. We really thought there was such a thing. Yes?

COMMENT FROM THE FLOOR: So far there hasn't been much discussion here of how other governments manage their affairs in the information age. Some of them are at least as progressive and advanced as we are and some more so than we are. It would be interesting to see whether other countries have felt the need to create as many agencies and as many bureaus as we have and seem capable of creating ad infinitum. I suspect that some of them are not proceeding quite the way that we are. I think that in the information world as well as in other parts of this Washington spectrum we will find some day that we are terribly over-organized and that we need a President or a leadership in the Congress to decide that a different order is required. I don't know if you gentlemen would agree.

MR. SAMUELSON: Well, that's our system. We have a very decentralized system of political power in this country, and every interest group wants its own subcommittee or agency. And even aside from the politics of it, there is a great deal of professional specialization. All the different professional groups or industry groups want their own advocates, and so we get splintered up in ways that perhaps other countries with a different political tradition do not. Barring major events that turn everything upside down, like wars, that isn't going to change. Take trade policy, for example. People keep talking about centralizing trade policy with a new cabinet level position or whatever, but if that happens that department itself will splinter into a variety of different fiefdoms. Then people will begin running around the department and going to other agencies when they don't get their point of view across. So I think the trend we have seen is inevitable, although some events, short of war, may superimpose a sense of reality on everybody.

But I must say I don't think it is the end of the world.

MR. KAUZLARICH: But it does lead to counter-intuitive policy decisions. If all of this globalization is taking place in an interdependent, interrelated economy and we are thrown back to making decisions based on interest groups and particular regional or other concerns, it--

MR. SAMUELSON: True, but sometimes the decisions don't make any difference, because the world just goes along on its merry way and the decision makers are left looking back five years later and saying that policy did not work out the way they expected. I don't want to sound too cynical, because I'm not, but the world has a way of getting around things like that. Trade policy, for example, has in my opinion almost nothing to do with our trade balance. It is something that keeps us journalists and lawyers and consultants busy, but it has very little to do with actual trade patterns.

DR. GANLEY: May I comment on the question of how other governments are reacting to the decision-making process? I think other governments are becoming more and more like us. Look back to about 1976, for example, to Western Europe. The PTT's were essentially in charge of telecommunications policy then, and, except for a little bit of oversight here or there, nobody else cared about what was happening. Now, today there are many, many players involved in government and in the private sector. Everybody has different ideas. Nowadays the ministries of commerce and industry are involved, the finance minister is involved, the labor minister is involved. Even the prime minister is involved. Parliament is involved. The latest German draft law on telecommunications specifically limits the power of the minister of telecommunications. He must consult with the minister of economics.

This whole business of becoming more decentralized is for exactly the same reasons that we have decentralized here. As we discussed earlier, decentralization is being reintroduced in one form or another in most other countries that I'm aware of.

AMBASSADOR TUTHILL: Thank you.

AMBASSADOR BARALL: We talked a lot about increasing international relationships, but there is an area, it seems, to me where the relationships cannot improve very much. I am talking about First World-Third World relationships. We have many institutions now that are supposed to help. UNCTAD, for example. But UNCTAD gives us the concept that every nation can select its own means to economic development. In the Third World there is very little choice. They are in many cases what we used to call one-crop economies. So it is not going to be easy for the Third World to accommodate all this. If it is difficult for us, it is increasingly difficult for them. How do they meet change and develop? And I am not putting all the blame on them. Our Secretary of the Treasury, if he has a coherent policy with respect to Third World debt, it seems to me is encouraging U.S. private banks to let the Third World borrow its way out of debt. I don't know whether that is a valid description or whether we have any better policy than that, but I would like to hear some comments.

MR. KAUZLARICH: The first thing we have to recognize is we are not dealing with a monolith in the Third World, if we ever did. There are enough developing countries who are in positions of considerable economic as well as technological capability to make us rethink the question of what does the "Third World" mean. You have Brazil and you have India and you have China.

AMBASSADOR BARALL: And you have Argentina, but there aren't many of them.

MR. KAUZLARICH: I'd be prepared to name others as well that have capabilities. I am not saying that they are going to be able to participate in the first rank of each and every one of these activities -- even a Mauritius which is able to do things in the textile area that were simply unimaginable a few years ago for a country of that size. But these are realities. You are obviously going to have problems in Africa that will continue. But an institutional fix, whether it's UNCTAD or something else, will not happen. There are people in the U.N. system in a time warp on economic issues who simply have no idea what is going on in the real world, and our friends in Geneva are the classic case of people who are frozen in the late 1960s and early 1970s.

We are not going to get into a dialogue with developing countries as a group in an institutional sense. I think you almost have to do it on a case by case basis. Whether the present approach to debt is the right one is another question. I think if we were growing, if we had economic growth in developing countries higher than it is today, borrowing isn't a bad idea. But what you have is low growth and borrowing, and that raises questions.

AMBASSADOR TUTHILL: We will now go on to the political-security issues with Mr. Raymond, the Assistant Director of USIA.

III: POLITICAL AND SECURITY ISSUES

MR. RAYMOND: Thank you very much Mr. Ambassador. I approach this perhaps a bit less as an ambassador would -- and many of you here are ambassadors -- and more as someone who has been looking at the process of public diplomacy and democracy building and their interrelationship. I think that the whole phenomenon of the information revolution brings those two features inevitably very close together.

A few general comments. In my mind the information revolution is the third great world revolution. We talked about Gutenberg. I go back a little further. I would identify in particular the agricultural revolution, the industrial revolution and the current techno-communication revolution. The current revolution impacts on every aspect of contemporary society. In terms of politics, it impacts both on our alliances and our rivalries. It certainly has many considerations for the political and security field.

The information revolution essentially has no bounds. As a result of the global communication revolution, we can see the circulation of an idea instantaneously to every part of the world. As my colleague, USIA Director Charlie Wick, often notes, in 1863 Lincoln's Gettysburg Address was heard by a few thousand people, and its coverage was on the back pages of the local newspaper. In 1963 John F. Kennedy's assassination received coverage in virtually every corner of the globe within a matter of minutes. As a result of the communications revolution and the speed that accompanies communication, U.S. and other leaders have to generate understanding and support of their policies at home and abroad on all key issues.

My subject in this seminar includes both political and security issues. Since security questions have already been covered in part. I would like to concentrate on the political. Briefly, however, regarding security, we have difficulty in controlling the flow of sensitive material in critical areas where matters of intelligence and national security are involved. Terrorist acts are affected by rapid telecommunications. For example, the recent TWA highjacking in Lebanon was exacerbated through manipulation of the world press by members of the terrorist group. The spy in the sky satellite offers both intelligence and challenges. Our adversaries can learn more about us, and we can learn more about them. This obviously opens up possibilities in the area of verification and gives us information on such events as Chernobyl, which was not reported in adequate detail. It also tells us about agricultural droughts. These are just a few specifics relating to a question which is worth separate treatment.

With regard to political issues, I would like to make several points. I do not think there has been a comprehensive study of the impact of the communications revolution on all our key relationships. Representative Dante Fascell, in a speech as part of the annual Abshire lecture series three or four years ago, urged that we create a public-private commission to examine the impact of this revolution not only on our foreign policy process but on our society as well.

In terms of the foreign policy process, it impacts on north-south issues, which have been touched on by several of the previous speakers, on east-west issues and on west-west issues. I think we have here a parallelism between the communications revolution and the age of democracy, and I would like to develop that point briefly.

There is a direct relationship, as has already been noted, between individual rights, economic dynamism and the ability to relate to the communications revolution. Although there may be some differences of view on this, I think the best way to maximize this revolution is to take advantage of the creativity and the ideas that exist in our political, economic, and cultural spheres. The global market place of ideas and that of communication technologies work very closely together. Some nations, as Bob Samuelson said, may not compete as effectively in this area, and they are in danger of being marginalized. This, of course, has serious political consequences as far as we are concerned.

In terms of the moment of history that I am describing and the idea of creatively moving forward, several points about the east-west relationship are worth considerable discussion. Closed societies do not intrinsically foster creativity, which is vitally needed to cope with the new communication age. We see this graphically in what Gorbachev is trying to do in the Soviet Union today. He is trying to energize and involve the scientific, technical, and economic elites in the process of moving their country forward. In doing this, of course, he will face an internal conflict between control and openness. And if the Soviets accept this challenge, will it change the society? That is an unknown, but it is a vital question.

I would like to share several reflections that I have from three days of conversation with 17 or 18 Soviets who came for discussions with USIA on information. Threading throughout the whole discussion appeared to be an impulse on their side to have more contact, to have more exchange, to share more in the informational field. An interesting comment was made to us by a member of the propaganda department of the Central Committee, who said, "Jamming is outdated." When I asked, "Why don't you stop it?" He replied, "We're thinking about this and many other phenomena." I am not suggesting that they are going to stop jamming, although they have stopped jamming our Voice of America, but they did imply that it was more expensive than the gains they were getting. Why? Not because they particularly want to open their society, but because they realize that their society is becoming increasingly porous.

I asked a young Polish television producer who visited me a few weeks ago, "What TV satellite signals do you receive?" He said, "Well, I'm viewing German and French and sometimes English television." He also commented that there were between 500,000 and 800,000 VCRs in Poland and that satellite dishes, which were originally made rather informally, almost illegally, are now manufactured commercially in-country and are available -- not widely, but available. There are several thousand satellite dishes in Poland. There are satellite dishes in Hungary. Three years ago when I was in Hungary I asked about the availability of satellite dishes. They are for sale, and one Hungarian told me with great pride that they had reduced the size of the dish to one meter and would get it even smaller.

Now, if one contemplates the possibility of a satellite dish smaller than one meter and if one gets rid of the parabola dimensions so it is flat, it can be hidden, if the Eastern Soviets still restrict access to satellites. In other words, East Europeans will have and use a dish with a good chance that the security authorities will not know. This, of course, would further erode the regimes' communication monopoly. With the satellite dish inevitable, the revolution there is moving forward. But the use of VCRs is perhaps going forward even faster. So with this "Swiss cheese" or sieve-like status in respect to outside communications, jamming not only becomes an anachronism, which some people, at least, are recognizing, but it implies that they are still operating from a different frame of reference. They claim to be open, and this is so obviously an area where they are not that they may make a move of some kind. I doubt that such a move would involve Radio Free Europe (RFE) and Radio Liberty (RL) immediately, but it might affect the present jamming of Deutsche Welle, Kol Israel broadcasts and occasionally even the Vatican broadcasts to the Soviet Union.

I would now like to turn to the question of what impact these developments, i.e. the communication revolution, have on how we do our business in the field of diplomacy. First, traditional private diplomacy is yielding to public diplomacy. Communication has added a new dimension. It affects many, political issues, ranging from terrorism to drugs, to an array of bilateral relationships. We need to have clear headed public diplomacy strategies for most of our international meetings and most of our international events.

One example of this approach was the summit meeting between the United States and the Soviet Union in Washington in December 1987. It was a successful summit, I believe, and I think one of the factors contributing to its success was the public diplomacy dimension. Work was started on that several months before the meeting took place. Indeed, we have been working for several months on the summit that is coming up in Moscow later this month.

To do this, it is necessary to have a number of elements in place. You have to have a clear definition of what the policy issues are. Public diplomacy and policy always go hand in hand. They are not separate. You have to decide on your themes. Very importantly, you have to have a clear understanding of what public attitudes are in the foreign country as well as in the United States. You have to assess the strategies of others. You have to report on foreign media trends. And then you have to develop an aggressive public affairs strategy to reach the foreign media.

An integrated action plan between public diplomacy and the policy community is the key. One has only to think about the impact of Mikhail Gorbachev plunging into the crowds on Connecticut Avenue and one realizes how effective public diplomacy can be. Now, why is it important that he play to the crowd? Because by doing so he affects western attitudes. Perception and policy are now moving closer together than ever before because of the communication age.

There have been a number of key instances where public diplomacy and policy have gone so closely together that public diplomacy has turned policy. An example I would cite is the neutron bomb campaign. We sought to deploy or to make the neutron bomb -- the enhanced radiation weapon -- available in western Europe. We failed. We failed principally because of the reaction that was generated by a very effective multi-faceted Soviet program.

In 1983 we were successful in deploying intermediate range nuclear weapons. We were successful in large part because of an effective public diplomacy campaign. It would be fair to say that Vice President George Bush played a key role. His trip to Western Europe in the spring of 1983 was a critical step leading to the acceptance by the Europeans of the INF weapon. Now, those who are interested in arms negotiations should reflect on the fact that if the INF had not been deployed in 1983, it is highly unlikely that we would have had a zero-zero agreement on INF between the United States and the Soviet Union in 1987.

Other campaigns where information strategies played a vital role would include Khomeini's very effective use of VCRs, radio and television, leading to the overthrow of the Shah. Uses to which the communications revolution are put are not always positive. I have described how Gorbachev uses the information procedures that are available to him, and this, of course, includes the television broadcast with Tom Brokaw before he came to the United States in December 1987. It means his broadcasts are seen throughout Western Europe. This public diplomacy effort by Gorbachev in the west is not made simply to play the role of Mr. Nice Guy. He has particular policy goals, and he is targeting on Western Europe in a number of key policy areas. His goals include splitting NATO. He uses several themes. One is that "we are all Europeans." Another is that Americans are remote from Europe. The Soviets also press for removing all nuclear weapons, including short range tactical nuclear weapons, from Western Europe. In his effort to underscore that the political process in his country is changing Gorbachev obviously hopes to lay the groundwork for receiving Western assistance in rebuilding the Soviet economy and gaining access to western technology.

My final point is that to accomplish the goal of adjusting ourselves to the new technological era and the close relationship between public diplomacy and policy, it is vital that we, as a country and as a government, recognize the importance of this synergism. This will have an impact on the way we do business in the government. At the same time, it is essential to have the resources to do the job. In this regard, Gramm-Rudman has all the earmarks of being a total disaster for foreign policy efforts. I am specifically referring to the 150 account, the foreign affairs budget. We are going to have to find some way to mobilize the American people.

The Atlantic Council in concert with others has put together a series of seminars focusing on these issues, and obviously it is an area where people who have served long in the foreign policy establishment can play a very important role. We cannot allow ourselves to end up in a situation where we are devoting increasing resources to the defense establishment, on the theory that we gain the stability essential to world peace solely through the defense side, without recognizing the "political" side to foreign policy and national security.

The key issue, in my judgment, is that after the defense balances are reached -- and they will be reached -- the struggle is in the minds of men. It is in the political field. And we are going to have to have sufficient resources to wage that struggle. Fundamental questions of resource allocation will have to be addressed. My hope would be that the necessary resources will be available for the foreign policy community.

In terms of USIA's budget, our Voice of America modernization program has had to slow down very sharply. I would note the same thing pertains to RFE/RL's modernization program. We have put together a worldwide television capability, but it is somewhat limited in funding. With the help of Senator Pell, we have tried to increase exchange programs throughout the world, and that has been vital. The people-to-people contacts generated through our programs are key to getting our ideas across and promoting greater understanding. The whole field of information and communication is under financial pressure, and we need help.

In conclusion I would like to quote some words of George Shultz, philosophizing about the future. He was reflecting on the age of democracy and the potential for the information revolution to open a fresh current of ideas to all people. He said: "Society must be open to the new age of knowledge and information. To resist it deadens hope of progress. Democracy is the best way to deal with the stress and opportunities of change. The free marketplace for goods and ideas is the best way to handle decision making. The global nature of change must be matched by political developments particularly the strengthening and the closer association of like minded nations." In sum, Secretary Shultz made a plug for an association of states, democratic states. He highlighted the synergistic interaction between science and technological advances and political, economic and social development.

AMBASSADOR TUTHILL: Thank you very much.

MR. PETER GALBRAITH: I will first resist the temptation, Mr. Ambassador, to respond to your comments about my employer, the Senate Foreign Relations Committee, except to say that you also need to have qualified people sent up to the Senate and that the Luddite in question in Paris was a Tennessee businessman who had no prior diplomatic experience. But that is a separate question. I want to discuss Walt's comments because I think they raise some very fundamental points.

First, I agree with your point about there being a sieve. There has been a sieve in information for some time. How else do you explain the enormous impact that John F. Kennedy had in Eastern Europe and the great sense of grief and loss there when he was assassinated? That impact had much less to do with U.S. public diplomacy than the content of what he did and what he stood for. The same thing applies to Lincoln's Gettysburg Address. It was spoken to a few thousand people, but the words, the impact of it, the message was a very powerful one and it disseminated. I think that as we approach the information era we are looking much too much at how we master the technology, what our strategy is for promoting some viewpoint and less at the content of what it is we are doing.

I would argue that the reason that Europeans and many Americans reacted badly to administration arms control policies is not that we explained them badly. It had to do with the content of the policy. I know the Director of USIA said, "Oh, if only the Arabs understood our initiative to Iran, the President's initiative to Iran, they would appreciate it." I think they understood it very well, and no amount of public diplomacy was going to persuade them that it was an intelligent thing to sell arms to Khomeini.

And I think we have overemphasized that aspect of it in promoting the technology. For example, Worldnet costs $30 million a year and we want to make it $45 million. The question is whether what goes across it is good and whether anybody is watching. Actually the most watched program is George Michael's Sports Machine in Italy, which features things like outhouse races. Is that useful?

I would suggest that there is a structural problem here in terms of our public diplomacy. Chairman Pell has outlined a scheme for reorganizing it, but it seems to me that one of the problems is that you need to bring this public diplomacy process of USIA, the information part of it, into the State Department so that it is part of a policy process. USIA's job isn't just to prepare a strategy to sell the policy, but to be part of shaping that policy as an integral part of the State Department. Then we need to get the VOA away from this business of being the voice to helping it be part of that sieve, like the BBC. I think everyone who travels abroad appreciates that American diplomats and foreign audiences invariably compare the BBC favorably to the VOA. Why? Because it is viewed as -- whether it is or not -- as an objective news source. Finally, regarding exchanges, they are extremely effective; they are old technology, people to people. It would seem to me they too ought to be separate, and the Chairman has outlined the program for this.

MR. RAYMOND: Well, my first comment is that I don't really believe that a spokesman for the Reagan Administration and a liberal Democrat are going to agree fundamentally on every single policy point of the last eight years. I would hazard a prediction that the new President, Democrat or Republican, will find it very beneficial to be able to communicate to the world on television. I would be very surprised if a political leader who works his way through the democratic process in the United States will suddenly decide: "I don't want think I want to communicate regularly on television to the rest of the world. I'll choose something as a means."

Now, as far as Worldnet is concerned, I don't want to get into an in-house debate, which Peter and I engage in constantly. But I do think that the British, the French, the Germans, the Soviets and others are going to be finding enough time and sophistication to deal with TV and that both the current administration and future administrations will find information packages which will be important to communicate to the world by TV.

With regard to John F. Kennedy's message getting around, certainly it did penetrate eastern Europe. What is different right now, I think, is the relationship of the technical revolution to the whole communications issue. It has caused countries to move forward almost in exponential fashion. In Eastern Europe, particularly, and in the Soviet Union you see a recognition of the fact that their countries, their societies and their economies are falling behind. You have economic stagnation and you have political ferment, a combination which is very difficult. It is not caused by the United States; I'm not suggesting that. But it is a fact that those societies and their economies are flawed. And in their effort to try to get their economies moving forward, I think this question of technology and the information revolution plays an important role.

Lastly, on the question of reorganization, this is obviously an issue that will be discussed in various fora or even here. Giff Malone has articulated on that in a book and an article in the *Foreign Service Journal*. My own feeling is that it is very important for foreign policy to be very closely related to public diplomacy. USIA cannot, should not, and does not operate independently from the Department of State. I think the Department of State should be effective in its articulation of public diplomacy and more active in it. Personally I do not think you benefit a great deal by tearing apart one organization so that you can strengthen another one. I think the key is to make the two organizations work together more effectively. And I think in that regard there should be closer coordination. When I was on the National Security Council staff we tried to create a public diplomacy coordinating mechanism. Possibly a future administration would like to try to tighten that up a bit more and operate it from more of an interagency point of view.

One panacea, which might be very controversial in this gathering, would be to launch a rather major interdepartmental rotation program, and I'm talking of about 30 to 50 officers from USIA into State and vice versa. I'm not saying this with any authority from the USIA officials; it is my own personal judgment. But I think that State Department officers should have more of a feeling for public diplomacy, and I think they may get it by serving in USIA. USIA officers should have more feel for the foreign policy process, and they might get it by being rotated to the State Department.

MR. GALBRAITH: I want to make one point about television, which I think just underscores the importance of it. Obviously television is the wave of the future. I have a friend in Paris who receives on cable every morning CBS Evening News from the night before. CNN is picked up in London. In fact, you can watch debates in the Congress. It's happening. It's happening through our free private enterprise system. And the notion that a government TV station could somehow compete with CBS, ABC and NBC is, I think, very questionable. I think the President will communicate through television without having to invest resource dollars in something that inherently will never be as good as what the private sector itself produces. Does that sound like a liberal Democrat?

MR. RAYMOND: It sounds like somebody who has a particular position, let's put it that way. I would like to add one comment. When you have an opportunity of calling in 30 of the key media or foreign policy opinion formers -- let's say in France, or Germany, or England -- and have them sit down for an hour and have a face-to-face interview with the Secretary of State, taking sound bites from that, if they want to, but posing questions to the Secretary, drawing points from the discussion and using them that evening either on TV news, radio or in the newspaper, I think that is an ability to articulate an American foreign policy that we have not had before. We could have done it by radio, but unfortunately a lot of people watch television rather than listen to the radio.

Now, this does not mean--and here Peter is obviously right--that increasingly you're not going to have CNN, CBS and others making their material available around the world. But I do believe that the ability to articulate an American foreign policy position is a basic difference between the commercial network and the governmental network.

QUESTION FROM THE FLOOR: Could you comment on the role of the United Nations and public diplomacy? Must it be so concerned with damage at this point that it can no longer be used as a very effective vehicle for promoting public diplomacy?

MR. RAYMOND: There is certainly an important role for the United Nations in various ways, but we have seen historically that the organization is more limited than perhaps some of its goals and ideals. It played a key role in some aspects of the Afghanistan negotiation. I think it will play a key role in some of the refuge resettlement issues. And there are many other vital issues. There is an important role for the United Nation in public diplomacy, but I think it is more restricted and more limited than we might have hoped many years ago.

MR. BURNS: I want to make one further distinction. Earlier I pointed out the distinction between communication and understanding. I think there is a another distinction: the difference between understanding and cooperation. It might very well be that a country would have total understanding and still for very valid reasons not wish to cooperate in a given area. Also, I think it is important to underline that there are many voices in America, and that is one of the strengths of the United States. Given the present proliferation and increasing proliferation of information, as you and others have pointed out, USIA and others are going to have to seek out comparative advantage. What can they provide that no one else can provide? In that context it would seem to me that being PAO in Canada would be the toughest job on earth.

MR. RAYMOND: I don't know whether that was a question or a statement, but I agree with the basic thrust.

AMBASSADOR WILLIAM KONTOS: This may not be properly called public diplomacy, but how does the U.S. government collectively begin to convey intelligently the rationale of American foreign policy to the American public? What are the ways in which the U.S. government can introduce a dimension of coherence and intelligence to the debate that is going on within the world of non-governmental organizations, within the world of trade unions and the churches? How does one tackle this important area, where foreign influence has a very significant impact on what happens in Washington?

MR. RAYMOND: Let me make two points. Effective foreign policy in today's world involves reaching out to a broad cross section of society, not just in the United States, but overseas as well. A diplomatic mission performing effectively today can no longer deal only with the diplomatic corps. It has to reach out to a whole series of structures, including the trade unions, the press, the churches, the parties in and out of office, and various elements that play key roles in the economy. One has to do this internationally, but one also has to articulate as effectively as one can domestically. This domestic effort should be carried out essentially by two entities: the Department of State and its Public Affairs office, with the Secretary, of course, being the principal spokesman; and the White House, through the President and his spokesman.

I'm not going to pass judgment on whether this administration has the people in the right places, because if you do it effectively you will have the right people in the right places, but there is a process underway. The Secretary of State does travel in the United States and sends his key people out to articulate policy. They do meet with world affairs councils and with the various sectors that you have described. Whether we do it effectively I will leave to you to judge, but I think the process is there and that there is an effort to have as effective an outreach as possible. For example, when I was in the White House, I used to receive a monthly printout of State Department or non-State Department spokesmen travelling around the United States, speaking on specific policy questions, and the audiences to whom they were speaking. They ranged everywhere, from universities to press conferences to labor groups to religious groups. The procedure is in place. I leave it to you to judge whether it is being done effectively.

AMBASSADOR TUTHILL: I guess we had better stop there. I wish to say a word in support of your suggestions. Regardless of what happens in the reorganization of the United States government, the exchange of personnel between USIA and the Department of State is absolutely basic.

III

THE MEDIA AND PUBLIC OPINION

III

THE MEDIA AND PUBLIC OPINION

HENRY TREWHITT, Chief Diplomatic Correspondent, *US News and World Report*

RALPH J. BEGLEITER, Foreign Affairs Correspondent, Cable News Network

BEN J. WATTENBERG, Author, Editor of *Public Opinion*, Senior Fellow, American Enterprise Institute

AMBASSADOR TUTHILL: I will introduce the first speaker on "The Media and Public Opinion", Henry Trewhitt, Chief Diplomatic Correspondent, *U.S. News and World Report.*

MR. HENRY TREWHITT: One of the advantages of the passage of time in our business is that one has lived through several cycles of communication, as communications affect the coverage of diplomacy and public opinion. Now I don't quite date back to the time of handwritten dispatches and the wireless telegraph, but I do go back far enough to recall those days at the end of World War II and immediately thereafter when moving copy from a foreign capital more often than not was a difficult process.

Some of you will know what I am talking about when I mention the old press wireless system out of Paris, which had a wireless network that extended throughout most of Europe. That was the central coordinating point for press dispatchers from throughout that region, some in Africa as a matter of fact, and they would come into the home office by telex or other means. It was a very slow process. That was also a time when censorship was still very much in practice in most of the closed societies.

Just think for a moment about what the communications revolution has done to that process. Although the Soviet Union does not yet permit us to use our little Tandy 200 to send copy directly over the telephone line from a hotel room in Moscow to my home office here in Washington, in fact it has been done in their incautious moments, when the telephone line was clear enough to carry the signal. That has not happened very often, but it has been done and it can be done. That process has forced most of the other totalitarian, semi-totalitarian, authoritarian governments with pretensions to respectability and a desire for development to relax. They have to. I can travel throughout most of the Middle East now with instant communication back to the home office. It has changed attitudes; it requires better knowledge; it requires more sophistication on the part of governments. Somebody suggested that it was a shame to see governments tailoring their public pronouncements to 45 seconds on television. But it is a necessity, it's a requirement now.

The process has had other results as well. Journalists must be more sophisticated. The day of the swashbuckling, trenchcoated drunk is long past. But apart from abandoning his bad habits, the modern journalist, in large part because of modern communications, has had to become better at what he does. Consequently you see in the international field far more sophisticated people, people who know their area -- specialists who may be as qualified in a region and in a given set of diplomatic/political/economic problems as the diplomats and the think-tank people who are dealing with that area.

Why is that necessary? For one thing it's necessary to remain parallel with the sophistication of the people you're dealing with on a day-to-day basis. But more important, I think there is a greater sophistication on the part of the reader or the viewer. Now those of us in print tend to speak disparagingly of television news, with the glowing exception of CNN. I mean that seriously. CNN is the greatest thing that's happened in a long, long time. But the fact is, and it's a problem we were talking about earlier, more people are better informed today because of television and because, God help us, of *USA Today*. I'm not a great admirer of *USA Today*, but the fact is it gets to people, and it gets to them with issues they knew nothing about before. Of course, *USA Today* is a product of the new technology in many respects. And CNN couldn't function were it not for the new technology.

There is a cross-fertilization process underway here, which means that a lot of people in Albuquerque, and Cleveland, Tennessee, which is where I happen to be from, now know a little bit at least about issues they knew nothing about before and could not have been persuaded to read about in the local paper, if the local paper were qualified and interested in trying to educate them. That to me is one of the most important products of the communications revolution.

I probably can provoke some of you by suggesting that one of the byproducts of the technological revolution in diplomacy relates to the diplomats themselves. The days of the stars in diplomacy are past. Diplomats are not household words as they may have been 25 or 30 years ago. This is true partly, I will suggest, because of the instantaneous nature of communications between the Department of State and the White House and the home office.

The process is much faster than in the past. The temptation for the Secretary, or some other official, is to pick up the phone and call his ambassador, or call the foreign minister and deal directly with him -- and this must be a tremendous burden on a diplomat who is sitting wondering what in the world has gone past him from time to time. And I know that happens.

It calls for a different style of diplomacy. It calls for closer communication -- or it should call for closer communication -- between the Department and the diplomats who may or may not be bypassed in this process, because heaven knows you shouldn't leave your guy turning slowly in the wind in Belgrade or in some other capital, although that happens, too. Now in the best of all possible worlds I suppose you would be able to utilize these miracles of modern communication, while exploiting also the talent of your diplomats in the field at the same time. I know that the record is spotty in that regard, and I guess I'm surprised, as a matter of fact, to be told -- and I think probably from personal observation I would agree -- that the quality of young diplomats coming into the Foreign Service is just as high as ever, and possibly even higher. I would have thought a different reaction would have occurred.

There is no way to exploit modern communications and the ability of diplomats, however, if your policy happens to be disorganized at home. If the policy is not coordinated, modern communication doesn't help a bit. But that really doesn't relate to what we're talking about here.

So I throw those things out and ask you whether I'm right about them.

AMBASSADOR BERNBAUM: You struck a nerve when you mentioned Ambassadors being bypassed. I was in Caracas shortly after the Dominican move, and I learned very suddenly at about 5:00 in the evening that my predecessor was on his way to see the President of Venezuela. I sent my deputy down to the airport, and by that time my predecessor had already arrived and was closeted with the President. So I called back home and said, do you fellows want my resignation? They said, cool off, cool off, this happened, we didn't even know about it ourselves. This is a White House operation. Well eventually my predecessor showed up at the embassy, apologized, told me what had happened, described the proposal that he had made. He had no briefing whatsoever. He'd made a proposal to the President, he said, that seems reasonable. And I said, okay, that seems reasonable.

So we went back to see the President. We worked it out. And the proposal was vetoed in Washington.

MR. TREWHITT: Technological miracles won't help there, will they.

AMBASSADOR PETER BRIDGES: I just want to say, to begin with, that I think bypassing the ambassadors started before the telephone.

The second point is that I think the difference in telecommunications between, say, 30 years ago and now is not all that great. That is to say, an ambassador 30 years ago could send a good cogent telegram home, if he didn't send it by pouch. He can still do that now. The Secretary of State, if he wants to figure out where the foreign minister is coming from is not going to listen just to what the foreign minister is saying but what his ambassador is saying in place. And I think Secretaries of State tend to do that.

I did want to ask you one question. I think that most of us here will agree that the American foreign correspondents we have met overseas tend to be, as you say, very well prepared. They tend to be good students of the regions that they report on. I want to ask whether you think there are enough of them.

MR. TREWHITT: No, I don't. But I also understand some of the economics of the problem. The economics of journalism -- print journalism which I know something about, and electronic which I don't -- have changed to the point that the cost of maintaining a bureau is so enormous that major U.S. publications really cannot afford to maintain bureaus that are not going to produce material which is used on a more or less regular basis. We have discovered that in the last couple of years at *U.S. News*. We had some bureaus that were showing up in the magazine once a month, or even less. We can't afford a quarter of a million dollars a year for that. And that's roughly the cost that is involved. So that's part of the problem.

The *Times* is going back up again, I believe. They reduced the number of bureaus for a while, but I think they have been increasing them again. I don't know what considerations enter into that. Both *Time* and *Newsweek*, which have much larger staffs than ours, have been cutting back to some extent.

MR. RALPH BEGLEITER: Can I jump in on the economics question for just a second, just to give you the electronic perspective? I'll give you one example that illustrates the point that Hank is making. CNN has never covered one of the trips to Asia that Secretary Shultz makes every year in July to the ASEAN meeting and South Asia. We have never sent a correspondent on that trip. The reason is that the air miles are so expensive and the news value is so low. The cost of sending television crews to ten different destinations in Asia is enormous. You look at it and you say, "Yes, we'd love to have that story. But it's one story. It lasts two minutes on the air. Here's what we would have to spend to get it." And the ultimate decision is no.

So the answer to your question is, no, there aren't enough. But that doesn't help you get to where you can have enough. You have to face decisions realistically.

MR. TREWHITT: To come back to your first point, I agree that the facilities and the incentive ought to be there for the kind of communications you are talking about, but I've been around long enough to know that the temptation is such that the advanced technology does tend to encourage state departments to take shortcuts.

QUESTION FROM THE FLOOR: Mr. Trewhitt, what are some of the implications for a magazine such as your own in cutting back on the number of bureaus, foreign correspondents, in terms of accuracy, sophistication of analysis?

MR. TREWHITT: That's an interesting question. The news magazines -- and that's what I'll talk about to get at this point--are changing. And *USA Today* is one reason for the change. The news magazines are going to have to redefine their role. They were founded basically to supplement the news, to give people information that was not available to them before. That has changed, because of television, because of the surfeit of specialty magazines and because of *USA Today* and the fact that the *Wall Street Journal* and the *New York Times* are getting out there much more than they ever did before. We must adjust to that. We must not lose the news function, but we have to be able to present the material--and this applies to all three of us--in ways that are different, more appealing, more thoughtful, I hope more analytical and more attractive than in the past.

QUESTION FROM THE FLOOR: Isn't that a pretty tough order when you're depending on a foreign news agency or a stringer?

MR. TREWHITT: One of the things we have done is to improve the stringer network. We have some of the best local correspondents--including a lot of Americans, expatriates for one reason or another -- in a number of capitals in whom we have absolute confidence. And obviously the cost factor is much less. I suppose you can get yourself in trouble that way, but if you have good people here -- one of the advantages of a news magazine -- processing, writing and arranging the presentations and managing the analysis of the raw material that comes in from abroad, then you may be finding the formula that's going to fill that niche that I'm talking about. It has to be a different process. And there is no reason it can't be done.

AMBASSADOR TUTHILL: Let's go now to Ralph Begleiter, who is the Foreign Affairs Correspondent of Cable News Network.

MR. RALPH J. BEGLEITER: Thanks. One of the other effects that the improvement in information technology has, both in the State Department and in terms of transmittal of information between the U.S. and other countries, is that it cuts down the amount of time in which diplomacy has to work. There is less time for the cooking process, the thinking process, the development of a proposal.

The best recent example that I can think of relates to the Middle East peace process. Regardless of what you think of the Administration's proposal, think of the strain involved in trying to pursue a new Middle East peace initiative of any kind in an atmosphere that essentially amounts to a fishbowl. The instant the proposal is developed, it becomes public. The instant you change it, the change becomes public. Before you've had a chance to effectively communicate it, certainly not in person, between diplomats in the foreign capital, before you can even tell King Hussein what your change is, it's all over the airwaves, it's in the *New York Times* and the *Washington Post,* it's been analyzed in *U.S. News and World Report.* And then Hussein sees Shultz and Shultz says, well, you know, I'm sure you've read about it, Mr. King, here's the proposal.

I was thinking here of the London trip that Shultz took. But let's say you go to the region and you visit the Israelis. You talk with Shamir, you talk with Peres. Before you've even gone from Shamir's office to Peres's office, Peres knows all about it. The Israeli news media have it on their front pages and it's been on Israel radio. And because of that it's been picked up back in the U.S., and the American-Israel lobby is already reacting to it and has picked up the phone calling the State Department.

My point is simply that technology forces not only a change in the way you do business among diplomats, but it forces a much shorter time span on almost any kind of decision making. The Persian Gulf, for example. The Reykjavik summit is another excellent example of this problem. Reagan goes to the Reykjavik summit with a set of proposals, which the Allies know all about. They've been briefed. Shultz took good care of that. He comes out of Reykjavik and the Allies think they've been bamboozled, because they think Reagan went in there with something different. The communication is so rapid that the Allies have already formed preconceptions about what went on in that meeting room in Reykjavik before the diplomats have a chance to get there on the ground and, face-to-face, explain what has happened.

I think that is a serious problem that diplomats and journalists really have to take into account as they do their respective jobs. And

I'm not sure there's an answer. Time is shrinking. The time span for anything to work is shrinking. You don't have the time for the cables to go back and forth and the cooking to take place.

The same thing on a smaller scale occurs within the diplomatic establishment. And that is because of the development of the computer. The State Department is still laboring, in computer age terms, under a relatively ancient system. And yet people like Hank and me can dial into information services from anywhere in the world and get the very latest information that is public anywhere. In the State Department, you call up one bureau and you call up the other bureau that are supposed to be working together on some issue and you find out that they're two days behind one another on where things stand at the moment. They have access to the same information we have access to. But it isn't being used thoroughly yet. People are not used to the idea of having instantaneous source material available to them. Take the Gorbachev statement, the Shevardnadze news conference. There is no reason why a spokesman should ever have to say, well, we've just received the text and we're analyzing it. You didn't just receive the text, you could have received it at the same time I received it. It's there for the having. You have to find a way to get it into your shop, massage it, work with it, as quickly as it's available. So that's another challenge within the Department.

I'd like to touch also on pooling of coverage. Someone raised the question of whether it affects the analysis of a news correspondent's report if you don't have your own correspondent there. All of us, the print people as well as the broadcasters, are becoming more and more involved in what amounts to pool coverage. You have your correspondents because of what's between their ears. They don't have to be there any more in Moscow, in Geneva, in Jerusalem, to stand in front of the Prime Minister's office with a microphone and say, what do you think about this, Mr. Prime Minister? Now I think there is some value in being able to ask the Prime Minister the question, but you can accomplish a lot by listening to the answers and not having to waste those four or five hours and the travel time to be there to hear them. What you need the correspondents for is to analyze the raw material from the field and to conduct interviews when possible with the principals involved in a story. And the principals sometimes are not necessarily on the scene. You may be doing interviews in Moscow to cover the Middle East peace process that would be more valuable to you than traipsing around with the Secretary of State between Amman, Damascus and Jerusalem.

It's essentially a pooling of coverage. You are gathering raw material from different sources, you're using your correspondent and analysts' brains to process it, to figure out what kind of sense to make of it. I'm not sure that's necessarily a bad thing.

MR. TREWHITT: Relating to that, I made an argument that our magazine probably should cover the summit this time, with me doing it. I'll be doing one of the main narrative pieces, remaining here in the Washington office, taking reporting from our correspondents and perhaps stealing a direct quotation from CNN from time to time. In other words, the information available would be more complete and more suited to the role I was talking about earlier for the news magazines by my remaining in Washington. Incidentally, I lost that argument.

MR. BEGLEITER: Another point I wanted to make about correspondents and their access to the public, relates to public opinion. We are obviously the funnel of information to form public opinion. Somebody asked, is there enough coverage? I think the answer is no. If you look at the television newscasts, you will see a very small percentage of reporting devoted to international affairs. If you look in the newspapers, with the exception of the few large newspapers who make it a business to cover the world, and even they do so mostly on Sundays when there's a big advertising hole, which creates a bigger news hole, by and large you will find a fairly skimpy amount of international coverage. And each of you who has been in a post somewhere will look at a story and say, well, they should have explained that. It's only got one paragraph on this issue; I've been spending six months trying to get this issue across here. That's a problem. I don't see that situation improving at all. The only way to increase the volume of material available to the public is to get the public to have access to the same kinds of information sources we have. And that, I think, is a computer function. People are going to have to be taught to use their television sets and their computers at home to access databases on subjects that they're interested in, and to read the material. So much material out there is going unread. So I'm not sure whether the problem that we all perceive of publics not understanding international affairs is one that we can bear total responsibility for. The public has to show some interest. We don't give them enough; we don't force feed them enough. If the public wants to be well informed, it's going to have to make an effort.

One other point I want to make concerns the relationship between reporters and diplomats. I think that many diplomats, particularly experienced diplomats, recognize the importance of shaping public opinion, shaping a consensus on a foreign policy issue by making available to reporters the truth about a story. Otherwise a vacuum is created, and the reporter is going to go off and write whatever he wants to write.

COMMENT FROM THE FLOOR: Besides, you're a good source of information.

MR. BEGLEITER: Okay. And there are probably times, quite right, when there is a little bit of two-way street involved. We have a mutual interest, people in the government and people in the media, in educating the public and seeing to it that the truth on a story comes out. There are some times when the government wishes the truth didn't come out right away -- let's wait another month or another week or a day, and then it can come out, but we don't want it out right now. That's where the tension comes in. We want it on deadline; you want it when you want it. I think that kind of tension is healthy and should not prevent a good, firm relationship between a diplomat and a journalist.

Finally, I want to point out that for many journalists it's a case of looking at foreign affairs through the frosted glass of, let's say, a bathroom window. You can see that the diplomat inside is brushing his teeth, but you don't know what toothpaste he is using, you don't know what color the toothbrush is, and you don't know if he's using his left hand or his right hand. You can see the shadows moving behind the glass, but you don't have all of the information to tell you exactly what is going on. So we publish reports based on the best available information. Naturally there are going to be some things in them that are wrong. We try to avoid that, but we aren't allowed to open that frosted glass. And to the extent that you, as diplomats, can help us find out what color the toothpaste is, that's the extent to which our reports are going to be accurate. Otherwise we are not going to leave the front page empty, we are not going to start the broadcast by saying there wasn't any news today. We are going to say something about what we think is happening behind the frosted glass, and that's where the errors and the corrections and the changes in stories and changes in nuance come from.

AMBASSADOR TUTHILL: Thank you. We will now hear from Ben Wattenberg.

MR. BEN WATTENBERG, JR.: I wrote a book a few years ago called *The Good News Is The Bad News Is Wrong.* And as I was thinking through this topic about the new information technology, it occurred to me that the good news is that the new technology can spread the word; and the bad news is that the new technology can spread the word.

It's a mixed picture. What we are talking about is the power and the potency of television, which is really what is new in our era. And as we have seen in the United States, it is an extremely potent tool of information of a sort that the world has never seen before.

On balance, I think what it has wrought is good, but we ought to try to understand some aspects of both sides of it. It's good, I think, in this sense: It seems to me that the ultimate goal of American foreign policy is to expand, protect, defend, spread, Western values. That is more or less our game plan, as nearly as I've been able to figure it out. And we do that governmentally through USIA and through Radio Free Europe and Radio Liberty and some other instrumentalities. I'm on the board of the radios. But if you try to understand the way cultures and values are spread, it is obviously not mostly through USIA or Radio Free Europe or Radio Liberty, but through our media technology, be it movies or music or newspapers or magazines. And in the modern era, most particularly through television. The American television network shows are broadcast all over the world, with the possible exception of the Soviet Bloc countries. When you consider movies and television, and music to some extent, in the post-World War II years these devices have played an enormous role in disseminating a culture or a set of values. And that's to our benefit.

Now, in the past few years we have seen the spread of what is perhaps the most subversive machine in the history of the world: the videocassette recorder. There are already about 150 million VCRs in the world. You hear a complaint frequently about the VCRs, in the competitiveness argument that we go through periodically, that American engineers invented the VCR but the Japanese learned how to produce it better and that all over the world, wherever you go, there are Japanese VCRs. But that seems to me to miss the point. It is true that the Japanese have almost all of the hardware. It is equally true that the United States has almost all the software that is going into those machines. And if you are in the business of spreading values and trying to make the world safe for our values, for our way of life, for ourselves our children and our grandchildren, then what you are interested in is the software.

Now to use the VCR as an example, there already are several million VCRs in Eastern Europe and there are at least a million, and growing, in the Soviet Union. And you can ask, what are they buying? What tapes are they putting in those VCRs? We get reports from our research department at Radio Free Europe and Radio Liberty, and the answer is about what you would expect. People are looking first for entertainment, so they are getting James Bond and love stories and sitcoms and television dramas, and they are getting rock and roll. They are getting a lot of pornographic films, for the first year or two or three, until it gets boring. And they are getting tapes of movies like "Rambo". But they are also getting things like "Dr. Zhivago" and "Reds" and a lot of other sorts of movies. In Poland they are not only getting all of that, but they have been filming with an ancillary piece of technology, the hand-held low-cost, light-weight video camera. They are actually producing on a very low budget their own documentaries. Solidarity is doing it, other people are doing it, and distributing them around the country.

Now the truly subversive thing about the VCR is that if you have two of them and some blank tapes, you have the equivalent of a printing press. You can tape something off the air, you can get somebody to bring in the first cassette of "Rambo" or "Reds" or "Dr. Zhivago," or "Dallas" or "Dynasty" or a porno movie for that matter, and pretty soon you have a hundred of them. You give them out and soon they are all over the country. And unlike radios -- and I think VOA and RFE and Radio Liberty have done a remarkable job in the Soviet Bloc countries -- these are impossible to jam. They are having an enormous impact already in terms of spreading the ideas of the West, be they good or bad, obscene or beautiful. People are getting a sense of what the rest of the world is like in a way that they never had before.

And this is only going to grow. It doesn't seem to me that there is any real way of controlling it. The Soviet Union and Eastern Bloc countries are not trying to get rid of VCRs. They are in fact trying to figure out ways to produce their own that are as good as the Japanese. It will be a long day until that happens, but they are producing their own. They are not very good but they, work. So that's the good news.

The bad news, I think, in terms of the new media technology -- and it's by no means all bad -- is this. If you are a young diplomat perhaps going through the Fletcher School, or a young military officer going to West Point or the Naval Academy, and someone asks you what the most important military inventions of the last few years have been, you might say they are the smart electronics and smart weapons. But I would say that in recent years the most potent new military force is the lightweight television camera and satellite transmission, which has geometrically intensified the Vietnam television syndrome of people being able to see war in all its horror and see it immediately in living color.

Now what does this mean when you look at it in terms of an adversarial struggle in the world? What it means first is that non-free countries, be they Iran and Iraq or the Soviet Union, can wage long wars and that it will take a long, long time for them to pay a price to their own public. In those countries, unfortunately for their citizens, they are not getting TV coverage of the man on the battlefield showing the grizzly corpses and showing all the ugliness and horror of war. So they unfortunately retain the option, when they so choose, to use force as a diplomatic solution -- or as a non-diplomatic solution to what might otherwise have been a diplomatic problem.

We have seen in recent years that democracies can use force in certain cases, on an island or where it's something that happens very quickly. The British in the Falklands, far away, didn't allow any media in; in Grenada, the media got there a little late, by which time it was all over. However, if the events are on land and if they are at all protracted, it is very difficult to do something even minor. Consider, for example, the way the media covered the situation in El Salvador some years ago. We had, as I recall, a total of 50 marine advisors there. And yet there must have been 10 times more correspondents in El Salvador than marines. I don't know if you remember, there was a big story that went on day after day that the correspondents had actually found a marine carrying a rifle. Just imagine that. A U.S. marine carrying a rifle is against the rules of engagement. They said, "got you, look at this news!"

And then of course there was the terribly tragic situation of the four nuns who were killed. That was not really what the war was about, but it came to symbolize it. We saw those sorts of gory pictures over and over again. Given the very natural and wise reaction of the public in a free country to seeing the sort of grit and horror that is associated with war in their living rooms -- as we saw with Vietnam, but now more rapidly, and with more precision, with more gore and guts and what the television folks call "bang-bang" -- it is extremely difficult even to consider the force option. It is extremely difficult, if not impossible, for a democratic nation with a free press to use force.

I think the classic example, which military tacticians and political scientists may be looking at for a long time, is the case of Israel and Lebanon. There I think for the first time was a situation in which there was basically a free press in both countries. Israel is a very good assignment for a correspondent, Lebanon used to be a very good assignment. Everybody knew everybody there, you could jump into a Hertz rental car and get to the battlefield quickly.

In that war the networks had camera crews and correspondents on both sides. The reports were fed back to the United States via satellite, and you could show what, in fact, is a television producer's dream. You could see the Israeli artillery piece fire, and then you could see the round land somewhere and explode. So you had two bangs, bang and bang. "Here are the Israelis," the voice-over says, "The Israelis were firing on Beirut today." Bang. "And they said it caused great damage." Bang. Then the next cut was to Arafat in the hospital holding a baby, saying, here is this terrible situation.

I don't mean to trivialize it, because there was obviously a great deal of human anguish. Putting aside for a moment whether there was merit or not to that actual military engagement, the wave of negative publicity that the Israelis received made it politically impossible for them to consider that kind of force option again. Because of the impact of television. Whereas just a year or two earlier, I believe, in Hama in Syria, 10,000 people were killed, but there were no cameras. It's like the philosopher, Bartley. If a tree falls in the forest and no one hears it, did it really fall? If there is no television to record the horror which is going on all over the world, but we can only see it in free countries, is that really horror?

The new media equation comes out, I think, this way. It is very, very difficult these days for free and open societies either to use or threaten the use of force. Now we know that, and our adversaries know that, and they know that we know. And we also know that it's not very hard for them to use force. If we were just talking about the open democracies of the world, you could say that whoever invented the new television technology ought to get ten Nobel peace prizes, because it would be the greatest step toward the elimination of the horror of warfare, because free peoples will not stand typically for that sort of thing in their living room, once they see what it's like. But it's not the sound of one hand clapping; it's the sound of two hands clapping. We have an adversary who is not constricted by these sorts of media rules.

My own thought is that there is enough going on in the world other than this so that our side is winning the great contest. I earn my bread by the free press and I wouldn't trade it for anything in the world, including the negative, power politics aspects of it that I sketched out. But we ought not to simply say how wonderful the free press is without understanding that it carries with it some baggage that we really have to think about in the plotting of our diplomatic strategies in the years to come.

MR. BEGLEITER: Let me say on that last point that we are noticing there is some change taking place in that one-handed clapping. I think to a large extent the Soviet withdrawal from Afghanistan is the result of the Soviet people, and more of the Soviet leadership, becoming aware gradually over the last three or four years of the extent of the disaster that was going on with Soviet troops in Afghanistan. They certainly don't have a free media in the Soviet Union, but to the extent that reports were getting through, either from the West or from Soviet media themselves, there was an effect.

MR. WATTENBERG: I think your point is well taken. One of the many differences between Afghanistan and Vietnam was the method in which it was reported. Had the Afghanistan conflict been reported in the Soviet Union the way Vietnam was reported, it would not have lasted a year. And it lasted seven years. I guess all I'm saying is there is an enormous differential, even post-glasnost.

AMBASSADOR TUTHILL: You commented about the speed of information, the fact that while policy is being considered, it's already on the air. I would like to ask one question: Is this due to leaks or diarrhea of the mouth?

MR. BEGLEITER: I don't think there's any distinction between those two things.

AMBASSADOR TUTHILL: What I mean by diarrhea of the mouth is that the officials responsible talk, as distinct from a leak, which is usually produced by an underling who wants to appear to be important but doesn't approve of the policy.

MR. BEGLEITER: I'll stick with my statement that there is not much of a distinction. It used to be called running it up the flagpole; now it's called diarrhea of the mouth. In many cases, the outlines of a policy are made available to reporters to see how it flies. There are some people who may say, "well let's not run this one up the flagpole", and others say, "yes, we have to because we don't want our guy to be embarrassed. We can always deny it if it hasn't been proposed yet." So to me that's not much of an issue, really. I think there is a lot of red-herring discussion of leaks, and this administration was involved in that for a while. It has calmed down a bit now, but a couple of years ago they were just running around chasing their tails trying to find out who was leaking. It turned out it was all administration officials. They ended up firing one of Shultz's top policy planners because he had called a reporter and released a telegram that an ambassador had sent to Washington. Well, if you are going to run around chasing yourself all the time over whether it's a leak or diarrhea of the mouth, it's not worth the effort. I think that the most important question is, are we getting out accurate information about the policy? If the information is accurate, it can stand the light of day.

MR. MICHAEL SCHNEIDER: I'd like to question both Ralph and Ben. What do you think the Administration loses if it doesn't react immediately to events such as the Gorbachev moratorium?

MR. BEGLEITER: The first thing it loses is a public relations advantage. I think you will remember, if you recall the post-Reykjavik summit era. For about six months after Reykjavik Europe was just aflutter with: Gorbachev is really moving, putting forward all these proposals. Look at him! Why isn't the United States grabbing this thing? Gorbachev really had an advantage for awhile by having spilled his guts about what he told Reagan and what Reagan told him. The U.S. was playing catch-up ball for a good six months. Margaret Thatcher in an interview we had about three months ago was still complaining that many Europeans think the Soviet Union was running with the ball on arms control. She had to keep pointing out that these were

Western proposals. The Soviets are now coming around to accepting them.

I think it behooves governments, particularly Western governments, to react promptly, to have officials think promptly about a statement made by the other side. Now there is a problem of time. You can't think so promptly that you give an off-the-cuff answer that turns out to be wrong. You have to consider your answers carefully. But you can't massage them forever. You have to find a way to take the public relations edge off your opponent's statement if you can, and do so right away, so that it is reported contemporaneously. Otherwise you have the Gorbachev headline in today's paper and the U.S. response two days later, buried on the inside page, pointing out that the Gorbachev statement was actually a restatement of an American proposal that had been made two years ago.

MR. WATTENBERG: I am afraid that's right. You do have to react, or in certain cases act, immediately on the public relations and the press front. I was just thinking about the Grenada situation. It may have been a wise military policy for a variety of reasons not to have any press reporting coming out of Grenada. But what we have seen is that the press is in a mind-set now, and if they are not let in on the action early that becomes a big part of the story. You can take a successful operation and end up with the story page one above the fold about the press not being allowed in. So all of us in the press in one way or another have become very pampered. I guess that is probably good, because there is a lot of power here and it is a power basically of the people. But it places enormous obligations on the government to act and react very quickly, because that's the way the game is played now. And you can rail against it and say, but we need a week or we need two months to formulate a response.

MR. BEGLEITER: But those times are gone.

MR. WATTENBERG: That is exactly right. It is a new terrain, and you have to conform to the terrain. And it has been going on long enough now for everyone to understand. The first time around the track there were some excuses for American policy makers to say, well, we didn't understand. But when you see it happening again and again in administration after administration, you really have to come to the conclusion that some of those folks aren't very smart, because it is not that hard an equation to figure out.

MR. TUTHILL: We have a question.

MR. GALBRAITH: I first want to say that in the case of the Iran-Iraq War, actually they do cover those things rather closely. And all the blood and guts that are sold, particularly on Iranian TV, is considered a vindication of the justice of the cause, all those lucky people going instantly to paradise.

MR. BEGLEITER: They don't show the Iranian casualties as much, though. They show the Iraqi casualties.

AMBASSADOR TUTHILL: They show the Iranians, too, I've seen a lot of them.

MR. GALBRAITH: It can vary, but I think the point is basically well taken. My question is really to you. And it has to do with the U.S. government competition with the private networks overseas. The basic argument in favor of USIA's Worldnet broadcasts is that CNN, CBS, ABC and NBC, when they broadcast to Europe -- and after all you are picked up in Europe, CNN can be picked up in London -- filter the policy makers and that therefore there is a need for an alternative U.S. government television service to provide the unvarnished truth. I wonder if you have some comments about the quality of the Worldnet broadcast as compared to the private networks.

Second, whether that same result might not be achieved by making policy makers available to the Washington correspondents of overseas broadcast networks. And third, whether in spite of the effort to escape the filtering, since we can't broadcast directly to people, doesn't this, when it is picked up by the networks overseas, eventually amount to the same filtering process?

MR. BEGLEITER: I would like to respond to several points. First, the word "filtering" has a sort of negative freight to it. I want to turn it the other way around and say, that's my responsibility. The job of the fourth estate is to provide reporting and analysis of events around the world. And I will be critical of some of CNN's own coverage here.

Let me explain what I mean. CNN has a penchant for carrying things live. Live from the Kremlin. Reagan meets Gorbachev. And what you see in this live event is a beaming President Reagan and a beaming General Secretary Gorbachev shaking hands, and aren't things really great, we're having a hell of a summit. That is the live event. If you leave it at that, allowing the audience to draw conclusions from what they see, you are, in my opinion, ignoring a large part of the story that hasn't been presented live. For example, you are ignoring a human rights story that goes with it. You are ignoring the fact that Gorbachev just told Reagan, "No, we're not going to have a START agreement." And so on. So my point is that it is the responsibility of the news media, both American and foreign, to filter, to tell the public more than what is available visibly on the surface by just taking a photograph or carrying an event live. I don't see that as a negative thing, I see that as a positive thing.

Now from the government point of view, if I were the Secretary of State, I would say to myself, "Well, I want to get my point of view across and I don't want Begleiter to filter it. I don't want him to add the fact that I've been to the Middle East 20 times already and I still haven't gotten anywhere. All I want to say is that we're working hard at it. We're going to achieve results."

So from the government point of view, I think Worldnet is a terrific innovation. And I would like to see it succeed. I think now it is much, much too limited in its financial scope to have the kind of impact the U.S. government wishes it to have. But given a proper budget, Worldnet could be a fantastic news service. It would have to have two things, in my opinion. It would have to have an adequate budget, which it really doesn't have now, despite VOA's contention that Worldnet's budget is already too large and is sucking away from VOA. And it would also have to have the VOA charter.

I don't think the two will ever come together. I don't think the U.S. government will ever provide a government television network both the budget and independence to operate a truly useful service that would actually be carried and be made available to individual citizens abroad. It will always be excerpted, filtered by foreign journalists who do the same thing I do. They will record it off the air, they will take that little snippet of George Shultz, they will add it to a little snippet of Helmut Kohl, they will mix the two together and they will come up with what they consider to be a fair and balanced story.

In answer to your question about policy makers, making the policy makers available directly to foreign journalists would have exactly the same effect as letting journalists record it off VOA, or Worldnet, and then reuse it in their own stories. So I don't think there is any distinction between those two things. The problem with that approach always is, do you trust the journalists that you are making them available to?

Let me mention a little anecdote from Shultz's last trip to the Middle East that goes right to this point. On his previous trip he talked only with the American journalists who accompanied him. We got news conferences every day; we talked to him on the plane on background; we had all kinds of access. On the most recent trip, he discovered that if you really want to make progress in the Middle East you have got to convince some people that you are doing something. You have got to talk to the Palestinians, to the Israelis, to the Jordanians. And for that matter to the Syrians. So he made himself available and scheduled a number of interviews with local media. He appeared on Israeli television twice, in interviews with Israeli journalists to which we had no access. He made himself available to the Syrian news media, but the Syrian government refused to allow the Syrian news media to interview him. And he made himself available to the Jordanian news media; the Jordanian government did allow the journalists to have access to him, but after reviewing the tape decided they didn't want the citizens to hear it, so they didn't allow it to be broadcast.

This comes right to the point of what a Worldnet will accomplish. If you start from the premise that I start from, which is that it is a journalist's job to put things in perspective, to put things in context, then you have to conclude that you will never have direct access, the way the American president can command television time and talk directly to you and me as citizens. It is never going to happen abroad.

MR. WATTENBERG: Let me offer one little parochial sidecar to that. I am called frequently by some of the foreign press stationed here in the United States, asking me to do election commentary. "This is an election year, would you be the great pundit and tell us what's going on?" You could spend most of your week talking to the Swiss and the Belgians and the Japanese and the Malaysians. I am not in the State Department, and there is no particular bonus for me to talk to the people in Kuala Lumpur. And after a while you start saying no. Whereas if you are asked to be on Worldnet, there is a certain public responsibility and a certain private egomania that lets you say, sure, I will do it for Worldnet. From this one little perspective, it enables you to pool resources to get the people you want into foreign countries.

MR. LEE: I want to ask Ralph Begleiter whether this shortened transmission time and filtering have been accompanied by an improvement in objectivity or in the distinction between reporting and editorializing. I was thinking of two examples, just recently, that strike me. Now when Ollie North spoke at Liberty College, I think the media felt an obligation to point out that he was knocking down a straw man. He is actually being accused of something quite different from defending the freedom fighters. And the media pointed that out quite correctly. But then, for instance, in reporting on Mozambique, the *Washington Post* had a story on the Op Ed page about how Renamo commits atrocities so that apartheid may live and on the following day an editorial about "Pretoria's victims." Now it is like saying that every civilian land mine victim in Nicaragua is the result of deliberate instructions by the White House. We would resent that as unfair, and I think it's unfair in this case, too.

MR. BEGLEITER: My only comment is that I think anything goes on the Op Ed page, and ought to. Anything ought to be allowed on the Op Ed page. There ought to be more room in broadcast coverage for editorializing. It would free the news broadcast a little from the need to put too much context around a story.

I don't see any problem at all with pointing out Oliver North's creation of a straw man. That is the responsibility of the news media. As far as directing the implantation of every land mine in Nicaragua, the U.S. government claims a great deal of responsibility for its policy in Central America. And to the extent that it claims responsibility, it has to be saddled with responsibility. If it doesn't claim the responsibility, it will be able to shed that responsibility.

MR. LEE: I don't see the connection, that since the United States government accepts the responsibility, it should also accept the responsibility for every atrocity committed.

MR. BEGLEITER: We are getting now into a policy debate. There is certainly plenty of room on both sides of the Central America debate to question whether the policy is right or not. Pick any other country. When the Soviet Union invaded Afghanistan it had to take responsibility for the civilian casualties that were occurring there as a result of stirring up the pot.

MR. WATTENBERG: I want to make one point, backing up something Ralph said that I hadn't really thought of before: the need for more commentary on television. I feel it very acutely in print, writing a weekly column. These days the papers overbuy so many columns that you have to fight your way onto the Op Ed page even if you are a purchased syndicated column. That is because it has become sort of the conceit in American journalism that you run one page of columns. Now in Washington it's very interesting. Whatever you may think of the *Washington Times*, they run, I think, the largest Op Ed section in America, at least three pages of columns every day. I would not go so far as to say they are balanced right, left and center. But some of the people they have, including me, are very good.

But the point I want to make is this. People writing columns these days are not just journalists. You have a lot of people out in the intellectual world -- George McGovern writes a column, Julian Bond was writing a column, Norman Podhoretz writes a column, Jean Kirkpatrick is writing a column. You have a lot of people, both full-time journalists and public figures, writing once a week or twice a week, frequently spending more time and more effort on a single piece than a hard-news reporter is ever going to spend on it. Because they have all week and they have access.

I think what Ralph says about television is true in print as well, in that we would be better served with more opinion on our news, labeled as opinion, than having allegedly objective reporters putting more spin on the ball than Dizzy Dean ever dreamed of. It is not as if they don't have an opinion, they do have an opinion. And if you can make that dividing line clearer, if you get the context out of the news reporting and allow it into the commentary, it would be terrific. But on the network news you have, at best, one little 90-second shot of commentary.

MR. BEGLEITER: And the rest of it is loaded with innuendo.

MR. WATTENBERG: Yes. You have an NBC, you have John Chancellor. And on ABC you no longer have George Will; I don't see him doing commentary at night any more. And on CBS Moyers isn't there -- I don't think they have a commentator anymore. So you do not have opinion labeled as opinion by the basic network transmission belt of American journalism. And that is a shame in my judgment.

MR. BEGLEITER: That is related to a characteristic of network television that I think is a real problem. We all know what it is. All you get is 22 minutes a night. And if you were the guy that had to budget 22 minutes, you might think about throwing the commentary out, too. I think it is disgraceful in a country that has as much media as ours that we have only does 22 minutes a night of newscasting.

MR. WATTENBERG: Does CNN run commentary?

MR. BEGLEITER: No, CNN has a policy against running commentary. And that's why I was saying I think that there ought to be a place for it.

AMBASSADOR TUTHILL: One more question.

MR. RICHARD MONSEN: I was intrigued and encouraged by what Mr. Begleiter said about Shultz's last trip to the Middle East, that he did hold some press conferences and talk to some of the local press. My own observation over the years is that the State Department and Secretaries of State have been much more interested in domestic, American public opinion and what the American press said than about what the foreign press said. And it seems to me that maybe one result of the new communications revolution is that we have to become more aware and more attentive to foreign public opinion. But it has been a slow process, in my experience.

AMBASSADOR TUTHILL: I think we will have to end this session now. Thank you very much.

IV

THE CONDUCT OF AMERICAN DIPLOMACY IN A GLOBAL INFORMATION SOCIETY

IV

THE CONDUCT OF AMERICAN DIPLOMACY IN A GLOBAL INFORMATION SOCIETY

TOPIC I: PUBLIC DIPLOMACY
GIFFORD D. MALONE, former Deputy Associate Director and Acting Associate Director, U.S. Information Agency
WALTER R. ROBERTS, Diplomat-in-Residence, School of International Affairs, George Washington University
MICHAEL SCHNEIDER, Deputy Associate Director, U.S. Information Agency

TOPIC II: TECHNOLOGY IN THE SERVICE OF DIPLOMACY
MR. DAY O. MOUNT, Deputy Assistant Secretary for Information Systems, Department of State

TOPIC III: DIPLOMATIC PRACTICES
RICHARD N. VIETS, former U.S. Ambassador to Tanzania and Jordan

AMBASSADOR TUTHILL: I don't have to do much about this panel, because Gifford Malone is here, and, as you know, he is one of the organizers of this seminar. So I'll turn it over to him.

TOPIC I: PUBLIC DIPLOMACY

MR. GIFFORD MALONE: I would like to lead off the discussion of public diplomacy by indicating why in my opinion this form of diplomacy is particularly important in light of the communications-information revolution we are now experiencing.

First, however, I think a few words of definition are required. Public diplomacy has become a very popular phrase, especially within the Beltway. It seems to mean many things these days in the way it is being used. I will try to define it briefly, as I understand it, and I hope my colleagues will agree. If they do not, I am sure they will tell us.

The basic idea of public diplomacy is of course extremely old. It means that by communicating with the people of other countries we can affect their thinking in ways that are beneficial to ourselves -- and sometimes we like to think beneficial to them as well. Public diplomacy is sometimes referred to as government-to-people communication, and that is a pretty good shorthand description.

I think of public diplomacy as being separated into two fairly distinct elements, with two somewhat different but related objectives. I call these political advocacy and cultural communication. Political advocacy is simply an effort to persuade foreign publics that our policies are worthy of support. The purpose of cultural communication is broader and longer term. It is to help people understand us better as a nation, our institutions and our values, and at the same time to promote mutual understanding between ourselves and other peoples. I won't elaborate further except to say that in my view both of these aspects of public diplomacy are equally important. I don't see them as alternatives at all, although some people apparently sometimes do.

We have been talking here about a number of changes that the information age is bringing about in the world. I am going to indulge now in several generalities. This is an enormous subject, and I hope as I make these generalization that everyone will keep in mind some of the things that have already been said, by Diana Dougan and Bill Salmon, by Walt Raymond, by all our media friends, and by others.

First there is the perfectly obvious fact that we live in an age of unprecedented physical mobility of people. We have not talked much about that, but it is important. Another point that has not been mentioned, but that is certainly significant in the long run, is that literacy continues to increase. In many areas, of course, people are still illiterate, but more people in the world are literate than ever before. Then, we must consider the important changes that are occurring in the "high tech" area. We live in an era of instantaneous communication. An event anywhere is observable anywhere, provided the technology is there, and increasingly it is there.

Furthermore, the volume of information available in the world today is totally unprecedented, and it is accessible as never before in human history.

I don't think we are in a position to understand what all this means, but there are probably certain points we can agree upon. One is that there will be an accelerated interaction of cultures and social and political systems in the years ahead. I don't think there is any question about that.

Many of you may have read Michael Blumenthal's article in a recent issue of *Foreign Affairs.* Blumenthal, who lived in China as a youth, tells in the article of returning to China recently on a visit. He describes going out into the countryside and seeing a peasant watching a television news program on which President Reagan was being quizzed by the news correspondent, Sam Donaldson. The peasant was looking at this scene, apparently enjoying it and getting something out of it -- although what he was thinking we don't know. Blumenthal commented that the peasant's father might well have had no knowledge of the outside world beyond what he had seen in the next village. The world has become very much smaller.

A second point is that this interaction of cultures and political systems will be accompanied by a speed-up in political, economic and social change. How much we don't know. But certainly this will happen. Another point is that people are forming opinions today on many issues about which in the past they were totally ignorant. The effects of this process are also very hard to measure, but unquestionably there are effects. Who can doubt today that television is having a significant impact on how people are reacting to what is happening in Gaza and the West Bank, and on those events themselves? And one can make much the same point with regard to South Africa. People are forming opinions very quickly now, on arms issues, summits, Central America, and many other international questions.

Another point, which has already been made in our discussion, is that public opinion will be increasingly important in its effect on governments. And this includes the Soviet Union and Eastern Europe, parts of the world that we have traditionally regarded as totalitarian.

All of this, in my view, has direct relevance to public diplomacy. It means first of all that we have to give considerably greater attention than we have been accustomed to do, to explaining, clarifying, and promoting understanding of our policies. There is a notion in some quarters that with all the information available in the world, people can simply sort it out and come to their own conclusions. I believe that is an erroneous view. It is not one the U.S. government should adopt. One fundamental flaw in that view is that people have great difficulty in sorting out this mass of information. They don't know how to put it in context, indeed they may not be able to do so. And thus I think that organizing information, helping people to make sense of it, is an essential function of our government.

I believe, moreover, that public diplomacy -- and I am talking particularly about the advocacy side now -- needs to be an integral part of diplomacy. I don't think you can say that at present it really is. Effective public diplomacy cannot be just a matter of explaining our policies, even though that tends to be the way we think about it. Our normal practice is to do something and then try to explain it, put the best face on it we can. However, public diplomacy, if it is to be successful, requires that whenever possible we consider the probable effects of our actions, the probable effects of our policies on foreign public opinion, beforehand. We need to recognize that an action itself has public consequences, which may be very important and which in turn may lead to other consequences.

Now that seems so obvious that one wonders why it needs to be said, yet it is not the way we always behave. I think we do understand this point fairly well when it comes to summits or major conferences in which the President of the United States will participate. But it is hardly standard operating procedure.

Just to take examples from today's news -- and I don't know the answer to the questions I'm about to ask -- did we really think through what the effects on public opinion in Panama would be when we undertook our policies there? I don't know. I would not count on it.

We seemed to be very surprised when an anti-American demonstration occurred in Honduras recently. Had we really been thinking about public opinion in Honduras these last two or three years? I don't know. But I would suspect we did not. I raise these questions simply to try to underline the point I am trying to make.

Now of course I am not saying that our chief objective should be to please foreign public opinion in every case. Public opinion is just a factor we have to consider. And certainly we have to be willing to do things sometimes that we know will be unpopular. But the important thing is that we know. And if we do know and have thought about it ahead of time, perhaps we can mitigate the negative effects of our actions. Again, that seems pretty obvious, and yet I think it really has to be said over and over again.

A related point is that in the years ahead we need to pay more attention to foreign public opinion per-se, as distinct from merely making intuitive judgments about how countries will react. Public opinion polling tends to be looked down on by many American diplomats, but I think it is a useful tool and one that we can use more effectively. Of course some parts of the world don't lend themselves to polling at all; we all understand that. But others do. We have done more polling in recent years, but I think not enough, nor have we given enough attention to really sophisticated analysis of foreign public opinion.

There is also a relationship, it seems to me, between public diplomacy and the increasing interdependence of nations, which is itself a consequence of technological change. I would argue that conditions of interdependence require greater public understanding than conditions of isolation and self-sufficiency or imagined self-sufficiency. There are many issues of international concern that I believe will require a major effort of explanation and persuasion in the years ahead. Simply to cite one kind of example, I would mention environmental and ecological issues: depletion of the ozone layer, deforestation, marine resources, pollution. These are not, in my view, just intergovernmental issues. They cannot really be dealt with successfully unless people begin to understand them.

Finally, I want to say a word about cultural communication programs. The characteristics of the information age, it seems to me, make this aspect of public diplomacy even more important than before.

In a time of rapid change, a time of increasing interaction of people, it is essential to provide ways in which people can develop a deeper understanding of each other's societies -- as distinct from simply accumulating random facts and superficial impressions.

Cultural communication programs -- such things as overseas libraries, publications in foreign languages, book programs, imaginative use of television, and of course exchanges of people, academic exchanges, international visitor programs -- all of these are means to that end. They are important because they permit people to acquire knowledge and to interact in a structured way so as to maximize understanding.

And of course much of this is also a two-way process. It is obvious, I think, that Americans need to learn a great deal more about the rest of the world, a world in which so much activity and so many problems transcend national boundaries. Cultural communication programs help to do that, and for that reason they are particularly important in our time.

AMBASSADOR TUTHILL: I'm going to intrude just to make one comment about cultural communication. I thought when I left the Service of writing an article, confessions of a former diplomat. And this was not to be a confession having to do with booze or women or drugs, but about relative neglect of the cultural attache programs. The only bilateral mission I ever had was in Brazil. And I was very fortunate there because a friend of many of you here, Martin Ackerman, was the Cultural Affairs Officer. And Martin stood for no nonsense from the Ambassador. He dragged me into all sorts of things. And I have noticed in the Service, especially after leaving the Service, the tremendously effective results one gets from a careful selection of people who come to the United States.

When I was in various bilateral embassies before I got into OECD and the European Community, the rest of the embassy didn't adequately participate in the selection of these people. The Cultural Affairs Officer would come after you and you'd say, all right, all right. But the long-term effect, it almost always works. If you have a good selection you send somebody to the United States, you give him or her time to see America, to move in unofficial circles. Many of us in the State Department do not pay enough attention to this program.

Our next speaker is Walter Roberts, Diplomat in Residence, School of International Affairs at George Washington University. Mr. Roberts shares something with several of us in this room, namely he helped finance the Salzburg Seminar in its early years, in 1949 and 50. So we're delighted to have him here on the panel today. Not just for that but that helps.

DR. WALTER R. ROBERTS: Thank you very much. I had thought that I would say something pretty much along the same lines as my good friend, Giff Malone. But coming into this room here and seeing Ambassador Johnson and other very senior ambassadors, I thought I would start out by sharing with you an anecdote, a true one. In 1957 George Allen was appointed director of the United States Information Agency. He was one of the very senior Foreign Service officers, one of the original Career Ambassadors in the Service. Within a very few months, he sent a memorandum to Loy Henderson, who was then the Under Secretary for Administration in the Department of State, in which--he drafted the memorandum himself -- he recommended that the Bureau of Cultural and Educational Affairs (CU) of the Department of State be transferred to USIA. Thereupon, Loy Henderson called George on the phone and they arranged lunch, and I was fortunate in being invited by Director Allen to come along. While this was 30 years ago, I still remember vividly the conversation. Loy Henderson to George Allen: "George, I'm very surprised at your memorandum. You remember, when USIA was created a few years ago and Senator Fulbright and Senator Hickenlooper opposed the transfer of the cultural program into a separate agency, we sent out telegrams to a number of you in the field. You were then in New Delhi. And we asked you whether the information and the cultural programs ought to be separated. And you came back with one of the best memoranda. You said information and culture must never be put together again. And now, four years later, you are Director of USIA and you send me over this memorandum telling me that CU should be transferred to USIA."

George Allen listened, and then he said: "Loy, let me tell you a story." George Allen always had wonderful stories. "When Livvy Merchant" -- Livingston Merchant, one of the great Foreign Service Officers in our Service -- "served in Australia in the late '40s or early '50s, he wrote a memorandum in which he proposed that Australia and New Zealand, which were then part of the European Bureau, should be transferred to the Far Eastern Bureau. This went through the machinery of the Department and when Livvy Merchant was appointed Assistant Secretary for European Affairs in the first Eisenhower administration in 1953, one of the very first things that confronted him was a reorganization plan by the Department of State transferring Australia and New Zealand to Far Eastern Affairs. And he fought it. So the then Under Secretary for Administration pointed out to him, "But Livvy, it's on the basis of *your* proposal that we're transferring Australia and New Zealand to the Far Eastern Bureau." Whereupon Livingston Merchant said, "Yes but now that I'm Assistant Secretary of State for European Affairs I'm being more objective."

"Loy, I want you to know that now that I'm Director of USIA, I'm being more objective. CU belongs in USIA."

I'm telling you this story because this battle of reorganization and organization has gone on for a long time and will continue to go on. And why--and again I'm reminded by somebody who is sitting here with us, Jim Opsata, who wrote me the first letter appointing me in 1942 to the Voice of America--it's all because of historical reasons. We have an organization--and by the way I completely agree with Gifford Malone that there is a clear distinction between advocacy and cultural communication--which is based on historical facts. Before 1941 we were an insular power. We didn't think about projecting ourselves overseas. We didn't believe it was necessary policy-wise, we didn't think it was necessary culture-wise, to tell other people who we are, what our policies are. There was one exception, a small unit created in 1938 in State's Latin American division which dealt with cultural exchanges. But that was all.

Compare that with the British, the French, the Germans, all of them, for years they had information programs, they had press attaches overseas, they had cultural officers. I read the other day that a cultural section was created in the German Foreign Office as early as 1896. We didn't have anything. So here in 1941, the war broke out and we suddenly had to organize ourselves. And we began by placing intelligence and information in one office, we put black, white, gray propaganda in one basket. It was called Coordinator of Information, of which Bill Donovan was the director and Mr. Opsata was the executive director, if I remember correctly, at the time. And I was hired into the Voice of America, which became part of it, because of my Austrian background. I knew German well and so they hired me for the German language service.

Here we were and suddenly it dawned on us that we had a real problem. In early 1942, the British told us: "You handled this all wrong. Information and intelligence don't belong in the same category." So in the summer of 1942 the Coordinator of Information was split into two organizations: the Office of War Information (OWI) and the Office of Strategic Studies (OSS). Bill Donovan went with the OSS and Elmer Davis was appointed OWI director. I happened to sit in a chair which went with the OWI. Three years of war, we were in business: The Voice of America with many language services, information programs were started with overseas libraries, etc. August 1945: the war ended. In 1917 we had something similar, the so-called Creel Committee; it was disbanded at the end of the war. But in 1945, against the judgment of many people, particularly in Congress, we decided not to disband OWI. The domestic branch of OWI was dissolved, to be sure, but the overseas branch Harry Truman decided, well, let's keep them, give them a try in peacetime and let's see what happens.

And lock, stock and barrel OWI was transferred into the State Department. For the next eight years, till 1953, all of these activities were in the State Department. Most of the Foreign Service officers didn't particularly enjoy us in the State Department. And then came Senator Joe McCarthy, saying that there were two hundred-odd Communists in the State Department. And when you really pinned him down, he said that they were mostly in the Voice of America, they were in the libraries overseas. They peddled Howard Fast and John Steinbeck, and he regarded that as terrible. And so John Foster Dulles, when he became Secretary of State, was glad to get rid of all of us. Thus the USIA was created. And then, as I said before, Hickenlooper and Fulbright didn't want to mix up information and culture. So the cultural programs remained in State.

Now this is why the Department of State, unlike all the other foreign offices of the world, does not have a proper information program. The entire information program was transferred to USIA. What should not have gone over to USIA is what Gifford Malone called the policy advocacy. That should have stayed in the State Department. And if it had stayed in the State Department, everything would have developed differently. In the British foreign office, each Foreign Service officer serves as political officer, economic officer, administrative officer and information officer. Not in our State Department.

The State Department has not entered the information age. Mr. Shultz recently gave a great speech in which he said that the information age has replaced the industrial age. He is absolutely right. In the previous panel we heard that the State Department hasn't even technically entered the information age. Well I tell you, it certainly hasn't entered the information age substantively. If I were to hire a new Foreign Service officer, I would first look to see whether he is a good communicator, which means he has to be able to appear on television or before other audiences overseas. Look at how foreign ambassadors appear on our talk shows all the time, on Ted Koppel's Nightline and on the McNeil-Lehrer show. Everybody. Do our ambassadors do that overseas? No. Do our political officers do that? No. This is, however, what has to be done. The Department of State has to enter the information age. It has to become communications minded.

The role of ambassador has drastically changed. The ambassador today is no longer the eyes and the ears of the President overseas. He must be the mouth of the President overseas. He must be the one who communicates. He must go on television he must go to Council of Foreign Relations meetings overseas. He must go to universities, and so on. As Ambassador Tuthill said, I now teach at George Washington University. Every day I see on the list of speakers in one or the other department an ambassador who is accredited here in Washington or a political officer or an economic officer. This is what the Department of State should do. The Department of State must become a communications agency overseas.

Thank you very much.

AMBASSADOR TUTHILL: Thank you. Next we have Michael Schneider, Deputy Associate Director, USIA, in charge of programs.

MICHAEL SCHNEIDER: I was taken by the anecdote that Giff Malone told about the Chinese peasants in Mike Blumenthal's article. We will know the global village is truly global when one peasant turns to the other and says, "Do you know that Sam Donaldson wears a toupee?"

We are not that far away in terms of impressions and images that are part of information that people get around the world. But I fear, just as everyone else does who has discussed the subject here, that images are not the same as information, and information is not the same as understanding. We should ask ourselves how we go from images and impressions to information, coherently organized, to understanding. Furthermore, putting the communication process in the largest possible framework, how do we support the national interest? After all, what we are talking about in public diplomacy, as in every other aspect of diplomacy, is preserving and advancing the national interest. By the way, that concept for younger people is not something that is actively pursued and examined. Yet from the vantage point of traditional aspects of diplomacy, the concept of the national interest is something that we should all revisit and redevelop. The nation as a whole really needs to reexamine it also. One of the significant aspects of the information revolution is specialization and the decline of an integrated, nation-wide understanding of our global interests: fragmentation, the lack of coherence within policy making circles, within the executive branch and the legislative branch; the subdivision of power between the executive and the legislative branch; and a far more investigatory and adversarial press compared to the late 1960's.

I would like to recapitulate very briefly a couple of points that were made by this panel and by others earlier because I think they bear on some additional comments that I have. It is obvious that publics play a greater role in decision making than ever before. And by publics I don't mean mass publics. I think the concept of a mass public is unwise and inaccurate. Publics are various groups that are involved, as they see themselves, in the various roles they carry on in life, as consumer, as parent, as worker, as commuter, as whatever. Publics are more involved; publics are being involved by elites in and around governments. Governments and the circles of elites around them are mobilizing publics for advantage in the political process. Now I think that fact affects all types of societies, not just the democratic or industrialized democracies. It affects the authoritarian, the totalitarian regimes, open or closed societies of varying degrees. Leaders in even the most closed societies must today calculate the potential impact on their publics of actions that they want to take. They must defend against it or calculate the effect and then do something that will take it into consideration. Act or not act. Mobilize the public or not. That is increasingly a cardinal rule of decision making.

We in this country meticulously analyze the nature of public opinion and the role of publics in the political process, both with regard to the Congress and the executive branch. Everyone involved in the policy process carefully looks at who wants what, who believes what and how a certain action is likely to impinge upon which publics; and at what kind of involvement they will have and what the intensity of their involvement is. We do fall short a bit on measuring the indirect consequence of actions, but that is another issue.

The same discipline, as Giff and Walter have said, must apply within the executive branch, and it doesn't, not adequately. Research on and analysis of publics overseas is underfunded. We take the public into consideration sporadically, and quite often after the fact.

The information-communication revolution has had other impacts, of course. Secrecy is less viable than it used to be. Now that the French and others have a commercial satellite that can tell us exactly what went wrong with Chernobyl within hours, now that the media community is so actively engaged, now that technologies exist in the public sector and are no longer the preserve of the intelligence community, secrecy is less and less an option for any government, even the Soviet Union. Some of the ground rules -- not all of them -- will change. Some of the ground rules that apply in the West will affect the way even the most controlled societies do business.

Thirdly, as Ben Wattenberg said, television has been a central element of the information revolution. That is, impressions and sounds. It's not the kind of abstract logic that comes with reading print. We contend with a world that is increasingly revolving around and sensitized to these visual images and the combination of the sound and the visual. I see this most vividly in young children who read less than in the past and, according to a number of analyses, reason less, seek answers to problems more rapidly. Even the evolution of our office systems reveals a move away from print. The word processor you would think deals with print. Yet increasingly word processors are using icons to do business. The many cognitive changes accompanying the growing role of television in our lives has already and will undoubtedly increasingly affect the way diplomacy is conducted.

These are all necessities we must face. Ralph Begleiter and Ben Wattenberg, in answer to my asking whether it would not be nice if the government didn't have to respond quite so quickly in response to every headline, replied: But of course you do, and must. The demands, increasingly, on government leadership and on government across the board, are to react as quickly as the media to the headlines of the day. That skews the decision making process. That adds insult to injury, if you will. The "injury" is fragmentation or specialization that has come along with, and in some degree has been caused by, the information revolution within the administration. The "insult" is the need to respond always instantaneously. This process means that the lead time we have to think about issues and directions is further reduced.

If one is cynical or pessimistic by temperament, one would say we are all lost in a constant process of chasing after that ephemeral headline, that impression, that sound, that is driving us who knows where. And we don't really know where unless we can step back and take a look at something longer range, or some longer purpose or some larger concern that we have. I think we have all experienced it in our careers; I certainly have in mine. Quite often -- and it's particularly true in Washington -- we are driven by these pressures which are out of control. We cannot come to grips with these issues, yet the demands of the public diplomacy-public affairs process require us to respond to the day-to-day actions. Sometimes there is no opportunity to step back and get a sense of the larger picture. But in fact it is the larger picture, historically, which has somehow had an effect on the way nations behave. The impact on planning is clear. If we have a three-months plan we are doing well. Policy planners are indeed fortunate if their six-month or one-year or five-year projections can effectively be worked into the actual decision making process. This process is driven by the accelerated sequence of action and reaction, image formation that we all have to cope with in our daily lives. It's a real dilemma for us to face the paradox of having to deal with the daily world increasingly affected by the communications process itself, increasingly public, increasingly fragmented, increasingly incoherent, and yet take a longer view of where we want to go as a nation-state and as a society.

There are a number of points of view about the role of public diplomacy in support of U.S. interests. One stresses the inherent opposition of cultural and informational programs. I think to some extent we're dealing with the fallacy of the excluded middle. That is, I think the opposition that is posed between cultural diplomacy and political advocacy is exaggerated. They both not only have a role in the U.S. government, in the public diplomacy realm writ large, but they have relationships. They are complementary. And while they may work in different time-frames with somewhat different constituencies, with something akin to different attitudes and expectations, if you get down and analyze it and look at it, they are not really rivalrous, they are not really antagonistic. They are really parts of a larger process that we need to take into consideration.

By that I mean that information and advocacy, when done best, is open; is straightforward; is as honest and accurate as possible; is as tuned to the times as possible; is as responsive to the point of view of the interlocutor or the audience on the other side, whether it be an American audience or a foreign audience; is as sensitive to the cultural baggage, the trappings, the point of view, the concerns, the needs, the anxieties of that foreign audience as possible. Now those are all the attributes we sometimes say belong to the cultural community, when in fact they are just as necessary in the advocacy community if advocacy is to be successful.

Secondly, advocacy cannot be successful unless advocacy brings out, elicits the points of view, the attitudes, the arguments, of the other side. Because only by knowing that other side can one really advocate one's own side. In the process both change somewhat. On an individual level and even institutionally and nationally, when we interact with those societies in pursuit of our policies, or a broader national interest, we have to consider what their problems are and we have to -- we do in fact move toward some kind of common ground. And so do they. The advocacy process therefore is not one of sending messages to targets, it is one of interacting in the most fruitful way.

On the other hand, the cultural side, the cultural community and the cultural aspect of public diplomacy can indeed be very focused. I was in a meeting with French ministry of foreign affairs, ministry of culture and education ministry officials several months ago. We were talking about the French bicentennial, and they laid out a beautiful, coherent plan for their own revolutionary bicentennial in 1989. That was a focused use in the highest sense of culture for reasons of state. From an information and advocacy standpoint I was extremely impressed with what they had in mind. They were going to stress the human rights aspect of the French Revolution. It fit with their history, and it was a point of view or a theme that they wanted to get across. Focus must exist, whether it be cultural or whether it be informational.

The cultural community in the U.S. government -- the former Bureau of Cultural Affairs in the State Department and now the Educational Affairs Bureau of USIA -- has brought a cultural dynamic that has led to a longer range point of view, which is very salubrious for informational people. The informational types, those responsible for the advocacy programs, receive from the cultural community a broader view. It is the context which we talked about. It is the sense of where the other side is coming from. And it is a sense that there is something else out there besides the headline that makes a difference. So the combination is quite felicitous.

Whatever the organizational relations -- and I don't really want to go into that at this time -- these programs must be seen as parts of a whole, and they must be seen in support of the national interest. It behooves us all professionally, and it certainly behooves the nation, to recognize the downside of the telecommunications revolution as well as the advantages that it gives us and step back, insofar as we can, and to try to reestablish in a very substantive way a clear understanding of what the national interest is, and we might rebuild that sense of larger purpose called the national interest which will really take us into the next century very fruitfully.

AMBASSADOR TUTHILL: No cheering yet. Couple of questions. Way in the back, let's start back there with Bill Trueheart.

AMBASSADOR WILLIAM TRUEHEART: This is maybe a tricky one, but is there a role in advocacy diplomacy, a useful role for covert action?

MR. MALONE: I think there probably is, but I would be very loath to see the overt information side of the government mixed up in that. I don't know what the CIA does, but I think we can assume that there are certain covert activities that have to do with disseminating certain kinds of information. I guess there is a role for that type of activity. But even in the interest of an integrated approach, I would certainly not want to see that in any way get mixed up with what the State Department is doing or USIA is doing in this field.

AMBASSADOR TUTHILL: Anybody else amongst the audience want to comment on that?

AMBASSADOR RICHARD VIETS: This is all a matter of degree, and certainly is seen through the eyes of the beholder, but I'm not sure I find it any less morally or professionally ethical to use some covert action by a covert agency in this arena than I do the gross manipulation of the media by a White House press office or a State Department press office. And that goes on every day of the week.

MR. MALONE: I'm not really talking about ethics or morals here, but simply saying that I think the credibility in the case of USIA requires that a separation be maintained.

AMBASSADOR VIETS: It always has been maintained, so far as I'm aware of.

MR. MALONE: I think so, too.

AMBASSADOR VIETS: I don't think there has ever been an argument about that.

MR. SCHNEIDER: I would agree. I think the one essential factor that USIA as an institution must retain is credibility. So it will always be concerned about any allegations of covert action from others. And of course as you know overseas the word information translates negatively in many cultures, so we already have that strike against us. On the other hand, people take us for what they want, and people will deal with us in other societies. But it's more difficult for people to deal with us within their own political framework if the covert action label is pinned on the agency. So we are scrupulous in that respect, we have to be.

DR. SHERRY MUELLER: Ambassador Tuthill, I was delighted to hear your enthusiastic testimony, if somewhat belated, for the International Visitor Program. I work with the Institute of International Education's staff that relates to the USIA International Visitor Program, and we collaborate with USIA on about 500 international visitors each year. As all of you know, IIE is heavily involved with the Humphrey Program and the Fulbright Program. One of my concerns has been, as we all get captivated by the technology, whether there a is danger that as we try to meet these various resource needs -- as someone on the panel earlier talked about the resource needs of a Worldnet -- we will get so captivated by the technologies that we forget the value of the traditional exchanges. Also, is there a way to use some of these communications technologies to buttress or supplement the traditional exchanges? For example, sending a Humphrey Fellow home with computer time, telephone time, so that electronically somebody who has had the advantages of a face-to-face exchange experience can continue the dialogue. There is that elusive follow-up we always say we want and never quite identify enough ways to achieve. Could the panel please comment on that?

MR. MALONE: I think there is a danger that we can become captivated by technology. It happens all the time. Last fall the U.S. Advisory Commission on Public Diplomacy held an all-day conference. A very large part of it dealt with technology. Technology, although it's complicated, is in another sense easy to understand. Machines are doing things, we are sending messages, apparently communicating. And,yes, that is something the U.S. government has to watch all the time. But I think it is possible, nevertheless, to withstand the temptations.

AMBASSADOR TUTHILL: May I just make one comment on this. The revelation came to me, as you say, rather belatedly, but I think once you leave the Service and are mixed in with foundations and think tanks and universities, you see more of the evidence. And I would think you might give a little thought to the possibility of touching base with those of us who have left the Service and who have learned the success of this program. Any number of us would be delighted to document our own post-Service experience.

AMBASSADOR MAURICE BERNBAUM: I have a rather amusing anecdote about exchanges. When I was in Buenos Aires I had become friendly with the Under Secretary of the Interior, who never hesitated to tell me what was wrong with the United States. I finally said, look, this is nonsense, I'm going to send you to the States on a leader grant. So he went. And he returned and called me. We had lunch. And he said, it was a very interesting visit, you were perfectly right; I had all the wrong ideas about the United States. But, he said, I've got new criticisms to make.

MR. EUGENE KOPP: I'd like to supplement the very interesting history that Walter Roberts has pursued about the organization of USIA and CU and offer the suggestion that whatever is eventually decided about organization, the ability to implement it is going to be influenced by the personalities on the Hill who control it. Let's take CU. You may recall that the Cultural Affairs Officers were USIA officers and that their performance ratings and control of their activities were handled by USIA. But they were the executioners of the CU program of the Department of State. Now the history of that is a little bit cumbersome. First of all, as Walter correctly notes, Senator Fulbright had a philosophic attitude that cultural programs should not be tainted with information programs. There were, however, other members of Congress interested in these programs. One was Wayne Hayes. Wayne Hayes didn't have very many philosophical bones in his body, and his reason for keeping the functions separated related to certain, shall I say, extracurricular activities that he had, one of which preceded me at USIA and the other which I had to deal with. The former being a woman that he wanted a previous director to hire and the latter being a political crony that he wanted us to hire. And he absolutely controlled our ability to get funds and to make program decisions until he got his way.

On the other side of the House, you had Congressman John Rooney. Congressman Rooney did not feel that American taxpayers' money ought to be used to provide ballet dancers, as he used to say, for the enjoyment of foreign audiences unless, by God, it had a foreign affairs, hard-line anti-Communist mission. That stemmed from the fact that John Rooney's district was made up in large part of people from Eastern Europe.

I joined USIA in 1969. Frank Shakespeare was then the director. The only way Shakespeare could get any money out of John Rooney to support cultural affairs and exhibits was to assure him that no matter what the money was going for, it had a hard-line anti-Communist purpose. That situation relieved itself somewhat when Congressman Rooney passed away and when Wayne Hayes passed out of sight thanks to Elizabeth Ray.

I don't know what the situation is today, because I haven't been involved since then, but my point is, there are some very real political realities that people are going to have to take into account before deciding on what the next organizational status is for this whole operation.

MR. RAYMOND: I think a point that might be added to the question raised by Dr. Mueller from Institute for Intentional Education (IIE) is that there never will be enough resources. I think the USIA is doing its best to see to it that all kinds of cultural exchanges are in fact funded adequately. But it underscores a very real problem we have as a society. The way we are configured, I think the private sector must play an important role. Ambassador Tuthill has been involved in a number of organizations which I think are extremely helpful in that regard, the Atlantic Institute being an example, the Salzburg Seminar being another. And I think that one of our problems right now is that the philanthropic dollar, which used to be 22 cents or 25 cents on the dollar for international programs 25 years ago, is now 3 or 4 cents on the dollar. So I would hope that over a period of time there can be greater awareness in the private sector of the importance of these kinds of programs. And it is a public-private collaborative enterprise that is going to make this thing all work.

AMBASSADOR TUTHILL: Another thing, of course, which is greatly handicapping these private organizations, especially those operating in Europe, is the fall of the dollar. The Atlantic Institute went out of existence at the end of April, as you probably know, and the Salzburg Seminar is having a terrible time because of the exchange rate problem.

MR. BURNS: This is an excellent panel, and I think the questions have been laid out very clearly. I have one comment on Walter Roberts' plea that the Department of State political, economic and other officers give more attention to their role as public communicators and advocates. The problem probably can be solved if a Secretary of State insists that these activities be among the important criteria for promotion. At present it seems merely to be widely ignored.

One other comment earlier was that in a general sense many officers of the Department of State -- and it could very well be equally true for USIA -- are not really technologically or informationally literate. They are not literate even mechanically in terms of the information age. And that goes back to the general problem of scientific literacy, which I think we have tended to ignore. It is not given much attention in the promotion process. Now, the Service will respond if the promotion system rewards it.

DR. ROBERTS: I think, you are absolutely right. In the British Foreign Office, for instance, at this stage of the game they are not appointing ambassadors anymore who have not had information experience. Ninety-four percent of the present British ambassadors have had one tour of duty as an information officer. The present British information counselor in Washington was a previous ambassador, to give you an example. The former British information counselor is now head of a geographic area in the Foreign Office in London. The present German DCM here was a previous spokesman in the foreign office in Germany. So the interchange in other foreign offices exists. In ours it does not. I would recommend to the next Secretary of State to put that in. I think that will make the younger officers of the Department of State not shy away from information work but rather grab it.

AMBASSADOR TUTHILL: Let's have one more question.

AMBASSADOR BRIDGES: I wanted to raise a general question that I think has to do not only with what you have been discussing but also relates to what previous panelists have said. And that is, going back to what Gifford Malone was saying at the beginning, in a rather positive list of world factors, including literacy and others, he did mention in passing that the American people needed to know more about the world. I think that is a crucial problem and it lies behind much of the problem this government faces in the conduct of foreign affairs. My point is, what shall the government do about this, aside from the Department of Education? What shall the foreign affairs apparatus do about a public that is basically illiterate in world geography and tends to be so in world history and world economics?

MR. SCHNEIDER: For one, the Perkins Commission, which did a very thorough job reviewing language and area study capacities, should be revisited. The National Defense Education Act, National Defense Language Act, language and area studies, which are still on the books but not funded, should be revisited. Now this is probably whistling in the dark with all the budgetary problems that the United States has, but we certainly should take a look at the possibilities for new starts in foreign language and area studies and in some other basic ways to develop the knowledge of the world that all of our children and adults should have.

DR. ROBERTS: And if I may just add, I believe that since this meeting concerns the information revolution, I submit to you that today's listeners and viewers and readers are much better informed about the world than those 20 or 30 years ago. I think there is a vast improvement going on about knowledge of the world within the United States. And that is due to the information revolution, and indeed I give credit to the Department of State, to its domestic information program, which I think is doing quite well. You have on every one of the news shows at one time or another either Redman or Oakley, and they present the State Department position on the Middle East and so on. Whether you watch Jennings or Rather or Brokaw, you will be able to listen to the spokesman. I think people are much better informed today.

AMBASSADOR BRIDGES: I hope you are right. And I think you might be right as regards the more educated part of the American public, but there have been some studies that seem to show that at least at the elementary level people don't know as much as they used to about basic geography and basic facts.

AMBASSADOR TUTHILL: We have combined the two last sections of our discussion. Both have to do with diplomacy. The first, presented by Mr. Mount, has to do with technology in the service of diplomacy; then Ambassador Viets will discuss overall diplomatic practices.

TOPIC II: TECHNOLOGY IN THE SERVICE OF DIPLOMACY

MR. DAY O. MOUNT, Deputy Assistant Secretary for Information Systems, Department of State

Mr. Mount, who is the Deputy Assistant Secretary for Information Systems will lead off, and then we will have questions after both analysts have spoken.

MR. DAY O. MOUNT: Thank you. I'm really here mostly to listen, to take away perceptions and to learn from this discussion. One of the messages that is clearly coming through is that technology in the service of diplomacy is a strategic factor. I am an administrative officer serving in a function that the State Department has traditionally regarded as an administrative support function. And yet technology in the service of diplomacy is definitely a strategic factor for us, for our programs, for our reporting and analysis officers. I think that is gradually becoming more understood.

I would like to quote from a paper that was sent to the Secretary of State in September 1987. I haven't checked with the authors so I won't list their names, but it was a joint piece going from Policy Planning Staff (SP), Bureau of Oceans and Environmental and Scientific Affairs (OES) and Coordinator for International Communications and Information Policy (CIP). It indicates that the State Department has not yet entered the information age. The paper points out that this is in part because of inhibiting cultural factors, such as a preference for general or technical training and a bias towards doing business in a traditional, "old-boy" manner. It quotes an IBM vice president as saying that the State Department cannot understand or become a part of the information age until its members, senior as well as junior, use information technologies and directly experience their power.

That is where we come in, for my office offers technical capabilities for people to use, experience their power and decide for themselves how well they work.

I would like to hand out some briefing materials and quickly go through them and to provoke some questions on your part. These have to do with a system that the State Department has embarked upon called the Foreign Affairs Information System (FAIS). It is really an approach more than a single system. It is a way of approaching a very complex set of problems that State is faced with in terms of providing integrated tools to its officers.

There is a new concept in the government, and it is not new just to the government. In 1980 a law was passed called the Paperwork Reduction Act. It could have been called the Information Management Act of 1980. But it wasn't really understood in the State Department that information can be viewed and managed as an asset, like many other kinds of assets. Information needs to be managed, because if it is not approached that way the right tools to handle it are not developed. For example, in the State Department we initially looked at the manual processes of handling information, decided they were too slow and quickly speeded them up. We know from our own communications capability and many remarks made here, that it is possible to send information between two parties very quickly. In fact, if I give you all an electronic in-box, I can fill that electronic in-box up many times faster than I could fill up a paper in-box.

Most of the application of technology in the past has been to do just that, to speed the transmission of information from one point to another. And as suggested here, one of the results has been an information overload, and now a problem: What do I do with all this? How do I digest it? How do I handle it?

That should lead us to a realization that we really have to think about information as we do other kinds of assets, such as money and people, and think about it as a good that needs to be managed. We need to talk to the user -- the Foreign Service reporting and analysis officer, the Desk Officer -- and find out what kind of information they need, when they need it and how frequently they need it. We need to know what kind of public information they need, what needs to come in from the wire services, the Cable News Network, etc., or what kinds of information need to come in through State Department sources, such as our overseas reporting. We need to learn how quickly they have to turn it around, how quickly they have to use it, how often they go to source materials and do resource research or whether they rely mainly information from secondary sources.

Thus it is important to focus first on the information and not on the technology. The technology is always changing, but the real information needs change much more slowly. And certainly the capability of people to deal with the technology changes very slowly. We need to take a life-cycle approach to information, break down the life-cycle steps and do the analysis that is necessary to manage information. We take a life-cycle approach to managing our money, our households and our affairs in business. There is a life-cycle of information that must also be addressed.

The information life cycle includes the following steps: create/draft, communicate, use, maintain, recall, reuse, repackage, re-communicate, declassify, dispose. The words describing each step in the cycle aren't particularly important. That is, we can use different descriptors, but the idea is to view information from cradle to grave. Information is created somewhere and disposed of somewhere. It may be stored. For example, we have legal requirements to archive certain types of information in the State Department. One of the most important steps in the life cycle is the reuse of information. This might be cable traffic that has come in that can be excerpted from and used in a memorandum going to the Secretary. By looking at life-cycle steps we understand that we need to handle information in a form that can easily be transmitted and used and then reused, repackaged, presented in a different way, and then easily re-communicated.

The right perspective for those who provide the technology then is to see how it can support the steps in the information life cycle. If we are wise about the way we use technology, we can add value to the process by giving officers the tools that they need. Word processing is commonplace in the Department today, and approximately 50 percent of our information technology is devoted to word processing. Thus FAIS deals with text as its major component. I won't get into a detailed discussion of all the aspects of FAIS, but I wanted to share with you that we are trying to think about information first and then look at the way we apply technology. We know, for example, that the INR analyst has a different kind of problem than the Desk Officer in the Office of Central European Affairs (EUR/CE) and that as a result they need different kinds of tools to do their jobs.

Finally, there are two pages in the materials you have that are pictures, they are really functional pictures, to show you that we have thought about what happens to information from a functional perspective. What is important about this is that we conceptually approach the flow of information as integrated from user to user. We no longer can afford to think only of communications point to point, e.g. from an embassy to the Department. We have to think about going from officer to officer. It really isn't important to an individual who is sitting in Bonn worrying about getting election results back to the Department what technology is in between him or her and the Desk Officer in the Bureau of European Affairs.. What is important is that they have a certain capability. From our perspective in providing technology, what is important is that we integrate the systems that we provide so that we can support needs across the board, whether between ourselves and other agencies, between posts, wherever the need is. And as we are designing these systems, that is the kind of perspective we are taking.

The last page in the materials has some particular names which include one on the bottom called the DOSTN. That is the

Department of State Telecommunications Network. It is a modern packet-switch network for which we are now asking Congressional approval. It is a critical building block for us. Telecommunications, as we all know, has always been critical to the State Department. Yet these other pieces are also critical. The Central On-Line Retrieval Environment is a new system that we are designing to give better access to a very rich on-line foreign affairs database, with some 11 million citations of foreign policy documents going back to 1979.

The FAIS Bureau Process is in prototype in the Bureau of Inter-American Affairs today, with over 200 officers linked electronically to this system. In ARA/CEN an officer can send a cable out to the field by pushing a button. It goes out electrically without anyone having to get up and hand-carry it to the message center.

That is just a brief overview, maybe enough to spark some questions or some interest in our approach to technology.

AMBASSADOR TUTHILL: I think we will hold all the questions until we have had Ambassador Viets' presentation.

TOPIC III: DIPLOMATIC PRACTICES

RICHARD N. VIETS, former U.S. Ambassador to Tanzania and Jordan

AMBASSADOR RICHARD N. VIETS: I am going to make my remarks brief, and I am also going to be quite blunt. I am fresh off the griddle from the bureaucracy. However, all of the statements that I will make here I made once or a dozen or a hundred times while I was still on active duty, so what you are about to hear is not the confessions of a recently retired bureaucrat.

I might add, without being paranoiac, that I see that the subject of diplomatic practices takes a sort of hind role in this conference, and I wonder if that is not perhaps a metaphor of what the information age is doing to the practice of diplomacy.

I left the Foreign Service some six weeks ago in a somewhat depressed mood with respect to the capacity of the Foreign Service, and in a broader sense the foreign affairs institutions in this government, to come to grips with the implications of what we have been talking about here. I think that the combination of the juggernaut of technology, which has overwhelmed every institution that I have had anything to do with over the last 30 years, and politicization of the Foreign Service -- not simply the politicization of ambassadorial ranks, but also down into the lower ranks -- put me in a fairly pessimistic mood, a mood in which I remain.

I am old enough to remember vividly my first posting, which was as a Junior Officer Trainee in USIA in Kabul, Afghanistan in 1955. One of my tasks that year was to stand at the door of our adobe mud chancery and wait for the arrival, always late, of a tattered young man on a donkey from the PTT, bringing the overnight news roundup from Washington, which came in over PTT wires. The embassy had no outside communication with the world, with the exception of a little Briggs & Stratton generator down in the basement which the CIA used in emergencies. Otherwise we were totally dependent on the Afghan telegraph, an overland telegraph system.

You can imagine in the best of days what kind of garbage you would be handed. In the worst of days, it was simply an endless series of sheets of letters jumbled together. It used to take me two to three to four hours of quite hard work to make some sense out of what this daily unclassified news summary was all about.

Last week I was in Amman, Jordan, and at about 9:00 in the morning I was in the royal palace talking to a friend who had recently come back from a year at MIT studying computers and information technology. He said to me, as I was waiting to go down and have breakfast with the King, "watch out, His Majesty is very upset by a piece by Charles Krauthammer in this morning's *Washington Post.*" This was 9:00 in the morning in Amman; it was 2:00 a.m. in Washington the same day. And I laughed and said, jokingly, "thank God I am not our Ambassador here anymore so I don't have to worry about that." But I realized that here was another metaphor. The King of Jordan was reading the *Washington Post* at breakfast time, or late breakfast in Jordan, before anybody in Washington had even seen it, except those people who had written it, got it into the printing presses and on its way out to distribution. That is one hell of a problem today for any ambassador, any embassy, anywhere in the world, in a capital that has access to modern telecommunications networks.

In the case of the royal palace in Amman, not only do they get the morning *Washington Post* in four or five minutes, whatever these super high speed printers do with it now, but they get the *New York Times,* the *Wall Street Journal,* and the *Christian Science Monitor.* By the time our poor Ambassador gets up, has tuned in to the Voice of America, which is carrying yesterday's news, and has read his wireless file, which is carrying quite frequently day before yesterday's news, he has a problem on his hands when he receives that call from the royal palace or the minister of foreign affairs.

That is one quick example of what has happened in the traditional practice of diplomacy. The American ambassador, who used to be the king in the jungle in terms of the information which he had at his fingertips, now finds himself in fact almost at the end of the line. We are dealing now with governments that have been smart enough to tie into every single important telecommunications network available in this country, that monitor very carefully, if they are interested, everything we do, and that are frequently well ahead of us in their knowledge of the day-to-day events that take place not only in our capital but in our society in general.

One of the traditional tools that any ambassador in the old days could use with considerable effectiveness was a transcript of the daily press briefing from the Department of State, which he had in hand by the afternoon of the day after it took place. You had the official line and you could take that to the foreign minister, lay it on his desk and explain what it all meant. There are two points to make in this regard. First, I am afraid I am in disagreement with previous speakers, and indeed others here, who suggested that the daily press brief was somehow a gigantic step forward in the articulation of American foreign policy. I happen to think it is one of the biggest burdens that any mission abroad, and I would like to think anybody in this town who carries a little bit of foreign policy water on his shoulders, has to deal with. And I feel that way for the following reasons.

I don't know whether anyone here has ever had the pleasure of participating in the formulation of the answers and questions that the daily press briefer hands out to the unwashed masses in the briefing room at the State Department. In my judgment, it is a pathetic procedure. It starts very early in the morning. Somebody gets in around 4:30 a.m. in most bureaus and starts desperately going through those newspapers that King Hussein has already read (although that is irrelevant to the point I am about to make). This would normally be in the Public Affairs Bureau. By the time the spokesman or his deputy is in, there is on his desk a suggested list of questions. He runs through them and adds or subtracts, and people get to work on framing the answers. The answers, by and large, are of course produced by the same people who frame the questions. They will very likely pick up the phone, call a geographic desk involved, and get some frightened young officer who is scared to death that he may give the man drafting the response an answer that could get him in trouble. So he is going to give the lowest common denominator response possible in the English language. The public affairs fellow himself probably has not had any appreciable experience at the policy level in either the State Department or USIA, so he is more or less swimming in a miasma of unknowns. In any case, whatever is drafted finally ends up, in most bureaus in the State Department, on the desk of the senior Deputy Assistant Secretary. That official has probably got 4,000 other things that he has to get off his desk within the same time frame that the questions and answers have to move on upstairs to, guess who? The number two man in the Department of State. We have made great progress in this administration; it used to be the Secretary of State who went over these questions and answers. Now we are down to the Deputy Secretary of State. I think that the Deputy Secretary of State might have better things to do than to spend a certain amount of his morning going over "Qs and As" that the spokesman is going to use. I readily confess that there are moments when it is very important not only for the Deputy Secretary, but the Secretary and perhaps the President of the United States, to be aware of specific hot issues. But by and large, one would like to think that we have a professional institution in operation that could handle these things with a certain assurance that they are not going to blow up in anybody's face as soon as they hit the journalists' note pads down in the briefing room.

I might add that, to my knowledge, throughout this whole daily process very rarely is USIA involved. I find it almost criminal that the very people who are going to be asked to help carry the standard don't get involved on the takeoff.

My last point on the briefings is that the briefer himself, at least in this administration, is caught in the most terrible straitjacket. In consequence, not only are the answers themselves pat, for the most part, but the answers to the follow-up questions, which are usually tough and to the point, are an embarrassment for the poor man and an embarrassment for anybody who has to sit through these sessions. I am being very tough in making these points, but I think the basic message has validity.

A third element of traditional diplomacy which I think is being overwhelmed in the practice of diplomacy as most of us here have known it is information reporting by cable. It is being overwhelmed, in my judgment, by the excessive use of the telephone, both the secure line and the non-secure line. Of course it is a status symbol now for any officer to have a secure telephone on his desk, but if it isn't there, he will discuss the same information over AT&T, and it makes very little difference to him. I don't know whether any of you have ever had access to transcripts of conversations that some of our colleagues have over the international telephone lines. One wonders why the KGB manages to persuade its masters to keep so many people on duty, because you simply need to sit there with your network of ears and pick up a very great deal every day of what is going into the decision process in the American foreign policy establishment. That is particularly true, I am sorry to say, of my old institution, the State Department.

Another problem, which was discussed perhaps as much as was needed in the previous panel, is the near total lack of understanding on the part of our diplomats in general and our senior diplomats in particular of the importance of getting into the ring in the public policy field. Most ambassadors that I know are simply intimidated, to be polite, and I guess to be blunt are just scared, to get into the ring with journalists. And they, of course, are setting the pattern for their subordinates. So, many embassies turn to the poor press attache and say, "it's all yours, buddy, but don't say anything that is going to rebound on us." That is, in my judgment, a gross squandering of possibilities for the conduct of contemporary foreign policy. In my last post in Jordan, when things were hot there, I was spending an average of four to five hours a day briefing journalists. I did this myself, first, because I was the only person in the mission who had access to the total picture because of the sensitivity of the issues that one was involved in, and second, because I felt that if anybody was going to lose his job as a consequence of exploiting the press to the degree that I was trying to do, it ought to be me and not any subordinate.

I have to say thirdly, and this is the principal point I want to make, that we do very little in the way of training our young diplomats in this area. Very little. I recall last year Secretary Shultz got very upset, because he had seen an American ambassador on television and thought his performance was submarginal. So he put out an edict that all new chiefs of mission were to take a TV course down in the bowels of the Foreign Service Institute. And everybody trooped over and found there a fancy lady from Madison Avenue, who had an hour's fawning in front of the camera with them. And that was the sum total of the training for ambassadors to throw them into the front lines.

Lastly, I think that the whole training program for our Foreign Service officers, be they State or USIA, is in a near bankrupt situation.

I have talked perhaps more than you expected, and I have perhaps been even blunter than most of you expected. So I will leave it there and be willing to take any questions that you wish.

AMBASSADOR BERNBAUM: It seems to me that before a man becomes an ambassador, if he is a career Foreign Service officer, he does go through a catch-as-catch-can process. And as far as I can see, the ones who do survive and become mission chiefs are the ones who can handle this, regardless of the lack of training. Certainly most of the things that you are talking about have been part of my experience. And I never did have a feeling that I was lacking. I mean, I was picked because people assumed that I could handle these problems, and I assume the same thing applies to other mission chiefs.

AMBASSADOR VIETS: I think you would find, sir, that the process of selecting chiefs of mission today is a very different one than the one that you went through when you were picked for missions. What you are suggesting is entirely logical, but I don't think it happens to fit with today's facts. It is true, obviously, that the stars, wherever they are picked, will have this quality. It will either be an intuitive quality or be a quality they have been smart enough to exploit, train themselves in or found some other means of learning.

But we are picking a great many chiefs of mission now because we want to make sure that people from various parts of the Foreign Service, various parts of the State Department, all have a crack at being an ambassador. That doesn't necessarily mean that they are the best equipped. But we are very democratic in our consensual personnel policy.

MR. WILLIAM HAMILTON: A two-part question. For you, Dick, do you think the range of problems that you have spoken about so humanly and eloquently should cause the present Ambassador in Amman to wish that the Bureau of Near Eastern Affairs were in a lead position in having installed the system which Day Mount described? Is this going to be reassuring when these facilities and capabilities are in place?

And the second part for Day Mount. Is there a program in place or in the design phase to bring the cadres of today's Foreign Service to the point where they will rush eagerly to become part of this system rather than viewing its approach apprehensively?

AMBASSADOR VIETS: My answer may be somewhat outdated, as I haven't been on the receiving end of all of this for three years. But I can comment on my tours in the Middle East. Before I was in Jordan I was number two in our embassy in Tel Aviv. There you can imagine, given the fact that it was Tel Aviv and that there is an enormous Israeli information presence in Washington and an enormous American press presence in Tel Aviv, anything that related to Israel was immediately on everybody's desk. We used to spend tens of thousands of dollars week in and week out on the overseas telephone back to operation centers and desks at State and USIA begging the desk officers and the Op Centers to send us on the wire texts of pieces that the prime minister or the foreign minister would call about.

I am sure there must have been some improvement in that. Today I think some of it has become pro forma. But from my point of view, we ought to be exactly where King Hussein's young MIT man is. We ought to be able now simply to press those keys on a computer in Amman and pull up everything of consequence that has appeared in the five major newspapers overnight in the United States and everything of consequence that has been said on television. It's all there right now. And to have to wait for hours if not days to get it seems to be unconscionable.

This has nothing to do with the press, but it is a further example of what has been said throughout this session about how lethargic and how behind the curve we really have become in the Foreign Service. We all know that in Secretary Shultz's recent visit in Moscow, once the bilateral issues and arms control were out of the way, one of the key things he discussed with the Soviets was our Middle Eastern policy in an effort to hammer out at least the beginnings of a common approach. It took three days, three days, for the bureaucracy on the sixth floor of the State Department to extract from the bureaucracy on the seventh floor the most papish policy cable you ever saw to our ambassadors, eyes only, burn after reading, of what went on. Three days. Meanwhile, the Soviet ambassadors, to my knowledge, on the day following Shultzs' departure had been in to see the heads of state and heads of government of two countries, and maybe more, with a full read-out of the Soviet version of the US-Soviet talks. Here we are, leaders of the world and the information revolution. But we are in Model T days. Now that's not technology, that's attitude and that's practice and that's a lot of other things.

AMBASSADOR TUTHILL: There is a second part to the question.

MR. MOUNT: There are four "stages" in the introduction to technology. The first is fear, the second is ecstasy, the third is disillusionment, and the fourth is reality. A lot of our people are still in the fear stage and a lot more have started to go over to ecstasy, for instant access to information is being provided in a number of systems. But Ambassador Viets's comments are very well put. Ambassador Donald Leidel returned from Bahrain to do a study of our organizational capability to support modern technology. He had exactly the same problem in Bahrain, where he was scooped time and time again by a local capability which we did not duplicate.

Ambassador Leidel recommended a reorganization within the Department to really focus this effort and to build a new information resources management organization, which we are still moving towards at this point. However, the technology is expensive, there are problems in supporting it and problems such as getting public information mixed up with classified information. In the disillusionment and reality stages you begin to struggle with issues that don't have easy answers. But we need to struggle with them, I think, a lot more as we go into the future. To do that, we need a new organization.

One very positive thing that has happened is the development of a capability called Secure Electronic Mail. We have heard about the problem of using open telephone calls to discuss sensitive information. If you can sit at a secure FAIS terminal and you have the capability to use a keyboard, there is an option. For example, our Ambassador to Colombia was recently in the Department at a time when he had to make a critical decision about events that were going in Bogota. It was a classified situation, so I can't share the details, but it was critical that he talk to his Charge. He didn't want to go to the Operations Center to find a secure phone, because he wanted to be in the Office of Andean Affairs, where the action was and where he had the support of the people on the Desk. He sat down at an FAIS terminal and communicated back and forth in a fully secure mode with his Charge. Each Officer had a record of exactly what they had said; they did not forget something that might be casually mentioned in a telephone conversation. The Ambassador went up to the Assistant Secretary to get a decision; he got the decision he was looking for and then communicated the decision back instantly through secure electronic mail. Finally, he used FAIS to confirm the decision with a cable for the record.

That is one post out of many posts, but we are prototyping that today. This was very useful in a fast-breaking event. FAIS does not yet address access to public information, which I think is also very important.

However, in the Bureau of Intelligence and Research today there is a system which mirrors the White House system for communications. This does have access to the wire services. It contains a database so that officers can follow certain key events, by accessing an information profile. And you can get that instantly.

MR. KAUZLARICH: As someone who strongly agrees with everything you have said, there is one thing that I just cannot understand. We have been studying this issue for years, but we always seem to wait to develop the perfect system. There is equipment available now that will do a lot of the very basic things that Dick Viets was talking about, which are just driving people absolutely crazy in the field. There is no reason why you cannot get a very simple fax system and do things like get the morning press out to the field very quickly. We get so hung up on trying to create the perfect system that I think we fail to sit down and actually do something. I just cannot understand why people in other foreign affairs agencies can get together a nice little system for agency-wide information handling and the State Department cannot do it. I hope it is as simple as a question of budget. I don't see any technological reason why we cannot do what every major American business does and what other government agencies do. The question that really has not been asked here is -- whether it's the economic, or the communications policy or the diplomatic practice -- how does the United States exert leadership in the world in an increasingly complex, technologically fuzzy situation where there are countries that are more capable perhaps in some areas than even we are, and we are still struggling with the information environment of the late 1960's and early 1970's. I think we have a major problem.

AMBASSADOR VIETS: I would put a slightly different spin on the question. Are we better off as a consequence of having instantaneous access to this torrent of information and data? I seriously question, in the totality of it all, whether we really are. I don't happen to think that the analysis of foreign policy issues, either coming from the field or from Washington, necessarily is as acute as I certainly remember it was 20 years ago. That may be a reflection as much on people involved as it is on the access they have.

But secondly, I think it was David Burns who mentioned the fact that it is very difficult to drink from a fire hose. This is a splendid figure of speech, because any chief of mission abroad, to say nothing of the Secretary of State here and his senior staff, are today inundated with hundreds of thousands of words to plow through. An ambassador in a busy embassy today could literally spend all day long just reading cable traffic and still go home and it would be coming into his box. That was not true in the lives of some of those present here.

AMBASSADOR BRIDGES: I wanted to go on from what Dick was saying and suggest to Day that maybe in your list of the life cycle of information there are a couple of words missing. One is to monitor and one is to critique. I am not sure that is your job. It should be the job of someone like the Executive Secretary of the State Department. And without that I'm afraid that people will continue to be inundated. I always remember John Masters' autobiography. I always liked him because he went on to an interesting second career, and he's a pretty good writer. He said that when he worked with the general staff, in India, the chief of general staff said that every problem can be reduced to a paper not longer than one page and will be.

MR. BURNS: I want to follow up with a reminder of some of the technology that does exist and that potentially could keep the missions up to speed with the King of Jordan or Bahrain and at the same time manage the information flow. As Ambassador Viets said, it is all there. And it's there in blips. For example, the *Washington Post*, the *New York Times* and the *Wall Street Journal*, are all now available electronically. So the information does not have to be typed; it's there already.

Secondly, to get the information needed you apply Boolean logic. For example, if I am Ambassador to Jordan, I would like to see every article that has the word "Jordan" in it. Maybe nothing else, but just every article that has the word "Jordan" in it. Send that to me right away. It is possible to punch a couple of buttons to cause that to happen. It could be on the Ambassador's desk within minutes of it having been released by the publications. You can of course filter the process further, indicating what you want and what you want excluded.

AMBASSADOR TUTHILL: Just two more.

COMMENT FROM THE FLOOR: Dick, regarding instantaneous access to information, using the example of Krauthammer's article on King Hussein's breakfast table, it seems to me we have always been behind the curve. There has always been an AP press story ahead of us. It seems to me that the emphasis in your remarks should have been a little more on the selection of staff, selection of ambassadors. An ambassador should be able to tell King Hussein who Krauthammer is, where he is coming from, what the significance of the article is, and deal with the issue with a broad understanding of the American political scene and the underpinnings of the particular issue that is involved. It seems to me that you might have done us all a greater service if you had emphasized a little bit more what you started out with, namely, the politicization of the process, the way in which the choices are made, the whole dismaying question of recruitment of young Foreign Service officers and the lack of training. You touched on these things, but it seems to me that it was a part of your discourse which you might have elaborated on.

COMMENT FROM THE FLOOR: Your points are very well taken. All day long I've been sitting here reviewing my own past as I've listened to various speakers. And I think my bottom line is, so far as ambassadors are concerned, that irrespective of anything that I've heard today, nothing diminishes the need to get into place as the head of an American diplomatic mission overseas a person who is filled with good, solid horse sense and who is a very astute analyst of individuals. We can have all the instantaneous access to information that we want, but at the end of the day, if we have a President or Secretary of State who really knows how to use people, before they make that final decision they are going to say, well now, you know this guy. What do you think? We've read 40 million articles on him, but what do you think? And I turned in my grave listening to our TV people and media heros today saying how you can do all this sitting in Washington, using stringers and so on, and that we're getting more sophisticated than ever.

V

CONCLUSIONS

V

CONCLUSIONS

The discussion presented in the foregoing pages provides a broad look, supported by a wealth of detail, at the extent to which the communications revolution is affecting our lives and relations among sovereign states. The world in the information age is changing rapidly, posing new challenges with respect both to the issues we confront and the ways in which we must deal with them. One constant theme that runs throughout the discussion is the need to adapt our thinking and behavior to the demands and opportunities of this changing environment. This is the challenge for American policies and for American diplomacy in the information age.

Although the participants in the discussion made no effort to reach an agreed set of conclusions, the discussion nevertheless reveals a strong consensus on fundamentals and a considerable identity of views on a large number of issues. It seems useful, therefore, to recapitulate here some of the major points.

The first and obvious challenge is to understand this age correctly. In our time, as many panelists pointed out, we are observing a rapid breaking down of the limitations imposed by time and space and an internationalization of economic life that is much more than simply an increase in trade. Although this internationalism may be more generally obvious with respect to the world financial markets, it involves many sectors. Globalization of manufacturing has meant that production of product components is spread among many countries and that enterprises locate their facilities where conditions seem most appropriate. Modern communications enable them to operate economically and efficiently over vast distances. Similarly, many services can now be provided almost irrespective of physical location or proximity to the user. As a consequence, the dividing line between what is "domestic" and what is "foreign" is becoming increasingly blurred. These processes, as several panelists noted, are a force for decentralization, transcending national borders, and tending in various ways to diminish sovereign control by national authorities.

Governments face the necessity both of adjusting domestic policies to take account of these developments and of trying to reach international agreements concerning many issues that flow from them. The range of such issues requiring intergovernmental attention is broad, highly diverse and growing. The comments of Messrs. Kauzlarich, Leeson and Samuelson and Ambassador Dougan all underline in various ways the extent to which this is now occurring. In addition, in the communications field itself new types of questions are arising, requiring international accords on such matters as rules and regulations, standards, protection of privacy and property rights, and many others.

American policy makers and diplomats in the next decade and the next century will be faced with the need to develop sensible policies on a diversity of issues that are only beginning to be understood and in which in many cases the distinctions between national and global interests are not obvious. All of this will constitute a major test of the wisdom, imagination and farsightedness of the men and women called upon to manage our policies. It will require in many instances transcending traditional modes of thinking about domestic and international problems.

The second challenge is to adapt the conduct of American diplomacy to the new dimensions of the information age. The discussion produced numerous insights into this question; there is no need to recapitulate them here, but present-day diplomatists will find them worth reflecting upon. Several points emerged that probably deserve special mention. These relate particularly to the ability of the Department of State and of American diplomats abroad to carry on with maximum effectiveness in the new information environment.

One important question concerns the Department of State's capacity to handle the complex issues arising out of the information age and to perform well in its recently assumed role of government coordinator of international communications and information policy. The multiplicity of interests within the U.S. government makes this a formidable task. Given the number of government agencies involved, centralized policy direction is extremely difficult to achieve -- some participants seemed to think it impossible -- and State's coordinating function, and certainly its leadership role, in this area is far from being fully accepted. Whatever success it is able to achieve in managing this responsibility will depend to a considerable extent upon its human resources. If Foreign Service officers are in general poorly educated technologically and scientifically and relatively unversed in communications issues, as several of the participants asserted, the Department of State will be handicapped in fulfilling its assigned role, and U.S. diplomacy in this expanding field will not be as effective as it should be. The Department will tend to be, as Diana Dougan described it, a conduit for the messages and policies of other agencies, rather than a focal point for the integration of various interests. The panelists did not make specific recommendations as to how the department should remedy these deficiencies -- such as through training, changes in personnel recruitment or other measures -- but the discussion left little doubt that this is a matter that demands attention.

Another effect of the information age, mentioned by almost every commentator, is the extent to which it has increased the importance of the public aspects of diplomacy. While diplomacy has always had a public dimension, and it may be argued that the change is simply a matter of degree, the communications/information revolution has imposed, if not new, at least substantially modified requirements upon those charged with carrying it out. A number of conclusions flow from this basic point.

Four of the panelists expressed the opinion that consideration of foreign public opinion must become a normal part of the foreign policy process, not limited simply such things as the planning of summit meetings or a small number of special events. Public opinion exercises increasing influence upon governments in many parts of the world, and public perceptions can be decisive in the ultimate success or failure of a policy. Policy makers must pay greater attention to this factor now than in the past. An important corollary point is that they must have more and better foreign public opinion analysis at their disposal in fashioning their policies and deciding upon diplomatic strategies.

Overseas, public explanation of U.S. policies must be a matter of high priority not only for U.S. information officers but for American ambassadors and other members of their staffs. Public exposition of U.S. policies is hardly a new practice, but in the information age it has taken on significantly greater importance. Most American ambassadors engage in it to some degree, but many American diplomats are nevertheless not entirely comfortable in dealing with the press and performing as public advocates, preferring what they may see as the alternative of quiet, behind-the-scenes diplomacy. The seminar discussion strongly supports the view, however, that these are not alternatives, but necessary and complementary aspects of one process. U.S. representatives overseas must make use of the available news media to further U.S. policies, appear frequently on television and engage in other efforts directed toward influencing public opinion. Foreign representatives in Washington are often far more active in this respect than their American counterparts abroad.

Consistent attention to the public aspects of diplomacy will probably require some modification of outlook on the part of Foreign Service officers at all levels in the Department of State. The Department can do much to advance the process, but it will require thought and sustained effort. As Ambassador Viets noted, it will not be achieved simply by giving US ambassadors a few hours instruction on how to appear on television, however helpful such training may be.

The journalist participants in the seminar, supported by a number of others, emphasized that the communications revolution, with its consequent effect upon journalism and the transmission of information in general, has made diplomacy conducted in private far more difficult than it once was and to a considerable degree impossible. Much of what is communicated on a government-to-government level finds its way quickly into the public view. This imposes, among other things, an increasingly demanding requirement for speed in official commentary on events and on matters reported in the press. Clearly there are trade-offs between rapidity of response and the ability to render considered judgments, and these must be weighed in each instance. Nevertheless, failure to provide quick, authoritative statements can be detrimental to U.S. diplomatic efforts. Several participants in the discussion expressed the view that the Department of State should give more attention to this and find ways to improve the process in general. At the same time, as the journalists themselves stressed, diplomats are in a position to exploit the media effectively, and doing so can be of considerable assistance in bolstering U.S. diplomatic efforts abroad.

Current procedures and practices can undoubtedly be improved. Ambassador Viets set forth in critical detail his view of the inadequacies of the Department of State's daily press briefing process and its difficulty in providing official U.S. comment on fast-breaking issues. The panel of journalists pointed out some of the negative effects of such deficiencies. On the other hand, a system designed to produce speedy, substantive comment from the Department of State and its representatives overseas can bring dividends. It seems clear, too, as a number of the panelists suggested, that closer involvement of USIA officials in this process would be most helpful.

The discussion also underlined the desirability of the Department of State's making available to its ambassadors and other personnel abroad, as well as to its people at home, the benefits of modern communication and information technology. Many seminar participants expressed the view that the Department of State is not taking sufficient advantage of the technical possibilities currently available in the field of communications and information. The private sector and even some foreign governments are well ahead in having instant, on-line access to American newspapers, information retrieval services and other sources of information. Private corporations, it was noted, are in many instances better informed than our embassies abroad. Mr. Mount described a number of useful developments in the Department of State's internal use of modern information technology, but others suggested that there is a good deal more that could be done.

Overall, the need is for the Department of State and the U.S. government's foreign affairs establishment as a whole to grasp the possibilities offered by the information age to advance U.S. interests. This applies not only to employing modern technology and using the media to best advantage, but to recognizing the need to combine traditional diplomatic practices with public measures to achieve our national goals. There is today an understanding of these requirements in many quarters, as the seminar discussion clearly showed. None of this implies an abandonment of the traditional skills that have served our diplomats so well. It suggests, however, that more thought must be given to the changes that the information age has wrought and the many ways that our diplomacy can benefit from them.

APPENDIX A

APPENDIX A
LIST OF ABBREVIATIONS

ARA   Bureau of Inter-American Affairs, Department of State.

ARA/CEN   Office of Central American Affairs, Department of State.

ASEAN   Association of Southeast Asian Nations.

AT&T   American Telephone and Telegraph Company.

BBC   British Broadcasting Corporation.

CIA   Central Intelligence Agency.

CIP   Bureau of International Communications and Information Policy, Department of State.

CNN   Cable News Network.

CU   Bureau of Educational and Cultural Affairs, at one time a bureau in the Department of State.

EC   European Community.

EUR   Bureau of European and Canadian Affairs, Department of State.

EUR/CEN   Office of Central European Affairs, Department of State.

FAIS   Foreign Affairs Information System, Department of State.

Fax   Facsimile machine for sending images (text or graphics) over telephone lines.

FCC   Federal Communications Commission.

GATT   General Agreement on Tariffs and Trade.

IIE Institute for Intentional Education.

INR Bureau of Intelligence and Research, Department of State.

INTELSAT International Telecommunications Satellite Organization.

ITU International Telecommunications Union.

LANDSAT U.S. government-owned system for remote sensing of the earth by satellite.

NATO North Atlantic Treaty Organization.

NICs Newly industrialized countries.

OECD Organization for Economic Cooperation and Development.

OES Bureau of Oceans and International Environmental and Scientific Affairs, Department of State.

OSS Office of Strategic Services.

OTA Office of War Information.

OWI Office of War Information.

PTT Post, telegraph and telecommunications. An abbreviation used to describe a typical governmental organization, e.g. a ministry or department responsible for this general function.

RFE/RL Radio Free Europe/Radio Liberty.

SP Policy Planning Staff, Department of State.

SPOT A French commercial system for remote sensing by satellite.

UNCTAD United Nations Conference on Trade and Development.

UNESCO   United Nations Educational, Scientific and Cultural Organization.

USIA   United States Information Agency.

USTR   U.S. Trade Recorder.

VCR   Videocassette Recorder.

VOA   Voice of America.

WIPO   World Intellectual Property Organization.

APPENDIX B

APPENDIX B
PANEL MEMBERS
Biographical Sketches

John W. Tuthill, a Foreign Service officer for 29 years, served in numerous posts abroad and in the Department of State. He has served as U.S. representative to the OECD, with personal rank of ambassador, and also as U.S. Ambassador to the European Community. His last Foreign Service position was as U.S. Ambassador to Brazil, 1966-69. Mr. Tuthill has been associated with many academic and non-governmental organizations. He has been a professor of international politics at the Johns Hopkins University, Bologna Center, since 1969; Executive Director, trustee, with The American-Austrian Foundation, 1985 to the present; Director General and Governor of the Atlantic Institute for International Affairs; Member, advisory board, International Management and Development Institute; and Member of the Board of Directors, Institute for Study of Diplomacy Georgetown University.

Ralph J. Begleiter, is the Foreign Affairs Correspondent for Cable News Network, where his coverage of the Secretary of State and foreign events have led him to Asia, Africa, Europe, the Middle East and Central America. He has covered several international summit meetings, developments in arms control, the Middle East peace process, key meetings between the U.S. and Soviet Officials, Presidential Inaugurations and has interviewed world leaders such as François Mitterand and Margaret Thatcher. He has won three Associated Press regional awards.

Robert Lee Chartrand, is the Senior Specialist in Information Policy and Technology for the Congressional Research Service of the Library of Congress. Author of nearly a score of books and major congressional studies, he has served for more than 20 years, as advisor to members and committees of the U.S. Congress, on the roles and application of information and its technology within government and society. Mr. Chartrand held consultations with the Italian Parliament, European Parliament, Commission of the European Communities and the USIS missions in Rome and Brussels. In 1979 he conducted a series lectures and seminars for the United Nations Development Programme in the People's Republic of China.

In 1980 he contributed to the North Atlantic Treaty Organization AGARD review of information services.

Diana Lady Dougan, was appointed the first U.S. Coordinator and Director of the Bureau of International Communications and Information Policy in the Department of State, by President Ronald Reagan in 1982. In the fall of 1983, Congress established the position of Coordinator in statute with the permanent rank of Ambassador. As U.S. Coordinator, Ambassador Dougan worked closely with 14 government agencies in developing U.S. policies and strategies abroad. She was involved in the overseeing and representing of U.S. interests in multilateral forums such as the International Telecommunications Union, the Universal Postal Union and the OECD.

Oswald H. Ganley, is Executive Director of the Program on Information Resources Policy at Harvard University, where he also teaches at the John F. Kennedy School of Government. Formerly a career Foreign Service officer, he served as Deputy Assistant Secretary of State for Science and Technology, Director of the State Department's Office of Soviet and East European Science and Technology Affairs and as Diplomatic Consultant to the President's Science Advisor. He was U.S. Delegate to and Vice Chairman of the OECD Committee for Science and Technology, as well as Science and Technology Counselor at the American Embassies in Rome and Bucharest. He has been a consultant to the Under Secretary of State and an advisor to the U.S. Council for International Business.

Richard Dale Kauzlarich, is Deputy Director of the Policy Planning Staff responsible for economic issues. A career Foreign Service Officer since 1967, he has served as Deputy Director of the Department of State's Bureau of Economic and Business Affairs from 1977-1980. He served as Director of Department of State's Operation Center from 1983-1984. He was Deputy Assistant Secretary for International Economic and Social Affairs in the Bureau of International Organization Affairs from 1984 to 1986. Mr. Kauzlarich has also served abroad at U.S. Embassies in Addis Ababa and Tel Aviv as Economic Affairs Officer/Counselor.

Kenneth W. Leeson, is currently Telecommunications Advisor for the IBM Corporation. Previously he was Special Advisor for Policy and Director, Office of Policy and Planning in the State Department's

Office of the Coordinator for International Communications and Information Policy. In addition to his participation in bilateral discussions of telecommunications issues with the United Kingdom, Netherlands, Canada, Federal Republic of Germany, Mexico and Japan, he has been a regular member of U.S. delegations to the OECD's Committee on Information, Computer and Communications Policy. He has also served as delegate to the ITU's International Telegraph and Telephone Consultative Committee.

Gifford D. Malone, a retired State Department officer and Minister Counselor in the Foreign Service, served in both the Department of State, where he was senior Deputy Director of Management Operations from 1978-1980, and USIA where he was Deputy Associate Director and Acting Associate Director from 1980-1984. His service included tours in Moscow and Warsaw. He served in the Department of State's Bureau of Intelligence and Research and its Office of Soviet Union Affairs and as Deputy Assistant Director of USIA for the USSR and Eastern Europe. He is the author of *Political Advocacy and Cultural Communication: Organizing the Nation's Public Diplomacy* and of various articles on the subject.

Mr. Day O. Mount, has been the Deputy Assistant Secretary for Information Systems with the Department of State since July of 1984. His previous Foreign Service assignments include, Regional Administrative Management Center in Bangkok, where he was Executive Officer. He has served at two American Embassy posts in Athens and Vienna and has also served as Deputy Executive Director in the Bureau of European and Canadian Affairs.

Walter Raymond Jr., is Assistant Director of USIA, responsible for liaisons with Congress, the White House and other federal government agencies. He was assigned to the National Security Council as senior Staff member in July of 1982. He also served as Special Assistant to the President for National Security Affairs in the White House. He was Senior Director for International Communications and Information in the NSC, where he was responsible for staff coordination concerning public diplomacy as it relates to international information and communications activities.

Walter R. Roberts, is currently diplomat in residence at the George Washington University. Previously he was Executive Director, US Board for International Broadcasting. He has served as Deputy

Assistant Director for European Affairs, Deputy Associate Director for Research and Assessment, and later Associate Director of the USIA where he was awarded the Distinguished Honor Award. He has also served abroad as Counselor of Embassy for Public Affairs, American Embassy Belgrade and in Geneva as Counselor with the US Mission to International Organizations. In 1974-75 he was Project Director for the Panel on International Information, Education and Cultural Relations.

William C. Salmon, is Senior Advisor for Science and Technology to the Under Secretary for Security Assistance, Department of State, with responsibilities in foreign policy issues concerning among others, international communications and information policy. From 1982 to 1983, Mr. Salmon also served as Acting Coordinator for International Communications and Information Policy. From 1974 to 1978, he was assigned to the American Embassy in Paris, serving as Counselor for Scientific and Technological Affairs. From 1970 to 1974 he was Deputy Director of the Office of Environmental Affairs in the Bureau of Oceans, International and Scientific Affairs.

Robert J. Samuelson, is a columnist on Economics and Business for *Newsweek Magazine* and *The Washington Post.* Mr. Samuelson's column also appears in *The L.A. Times, The Boston Globe* and *The International Herald-Tribune.*

Michael Schneider, is Deputy Associate Director, Bureau of Programs, USIA. Prior to this position he has served as Special Assistant to the Assistant Director of Information Center Service. Mr. Schneider has also served abroad with USIS as Assistant Information Officer in Dacca, and as Public Affairs Trainee, USIS Calcutta.

Henry Trewhitt, is Chief Diplomatic Correspondent at *U.S. News & World Report.* In 1961, while working for the *Baltimore Sun,* he was assigned to the Bonn Bureau where he covered NATO, the EEC, East-West relations and the Berlin crisis of the early 1960's. He later joined *Newsweek Magazine* with assignments as Diplomatic Correspondent and White House Correspondent. He returned to the *Baltimore Sun* in 1974 as Diplomatic Correspondent until joining *U.S. News & World Report* in September of 1985. Mr. Trewhitt has traveled in more than 100 countries, has participated in two presidential campaign debates and is a frequent panelist on *Washington Week in Review*.

Richard N. Viets, a retired Foreign Service officer and Career Minister, was U.S. Ambassador to Tanzania and Jordan. He served in USIA posts in Afghanistan and Tunisia and in State Department posts as Commercial Officer in Tokyo and Madras as well as two posts in New Delhi. He also served as Deputy chief of Mission in Bucharest and in the same capacity in Tel Aviv.

Ben J. Wattenberg, is a senior fellow at the American Enterprise Institute in Washington, D.C. and co-editor of AEI's bi-monthly magazine, *Public Opinion*. He is also author of the current book *The Birth Death* and *The Good News Is The Bad News Is Wrong*. He has been host of two PBS television series *Ben Wattenberg at Large* and *In Search of the Real America*, (based on his 1974 book *The Real America*). In 1981 he was appointed by President Reagan to the Board for International Broadcasting, which oversees the activities of Radio Free Europe and Radio Liberty, and served as vice-Chairman of the Board.

DIPLOMATIC AND CONSULAR OFFICERS RETIRED
Dacor Bacon House
1801 F. Street, N.W.
Washington, D.C. 20006

OFFICERS

Claude G. Ross
President
Ambassador, Ret.

Joseph F. Donelan, Jr.,
Vice President
Counselor of Embassy, Ret.

Peter J. Skoufis,
Treasurer
Counselor of Embassy, Ret.

James B. Opsata,
Secretary
USIO, Ret.

William B. Cobb, Jr.,
Executive Director
FSO, Ret.

Thomas J. Corcoran,
Assistant Secretary
Ambassador, Ret.

BOARD OF GOVERNORS

Milton Barall, Ambassador, Ret.
Lucius D. Battle, Ambassador, Ret.
Robert H. Beers, USIO, Ret.
Maurice M. Bernbaum, Ambassador, Ret.
Eugene M. Braderman,
Consul General, Ret.
Richard P. Butrick,
Career Minister, Ret.
William D. Calderhead,
Counselor of Embassy, Ret.
Robert W. Caldwell, FSO, Ret.
Robert G. Cleveland,
Counselor of Embassy, Ret.
William A. Crawford, Ambassador, Ret.
Thomas J. Corcoran, Ambassador, Ret.
Joseph F. Donelan,
Counselor of Embassy, Ret.
Mrs. Herbert P. Fales,
Associate Member
Robert T. Hennemeyer,
Ambassador, Ret.
Carol C. Laise, Ambassador, Ret.

William H. Lehfeldt
Counselor of Embassy, Ret.
LaRUE R. Lutkins,
Counselor of Embassy, Ret.
Gifford D. Malone,
Minister-Counselor, Ret.
Allen B. Moreland,
Consul General, Ret.
David D. Newsom, Ambassador, Ret.
Mrs. Katherine H. Phillips
Associate Member
Robert J. Ryan, Ambassador, Ret.
Peter J. Skoufis,
Counselor of Embassy, Ret.
H.G. Torbert, Ambassador, Ret.
William C. Trueheart, Ambassador, Ret.
Richard E. Usher,
Counselor of Embassy, Ret.
George S. Vest, Ambassador, Ret.
Jean Wilkowski, Ambassador, Ret.
Robert L. Yost, Ambassador, Ret.